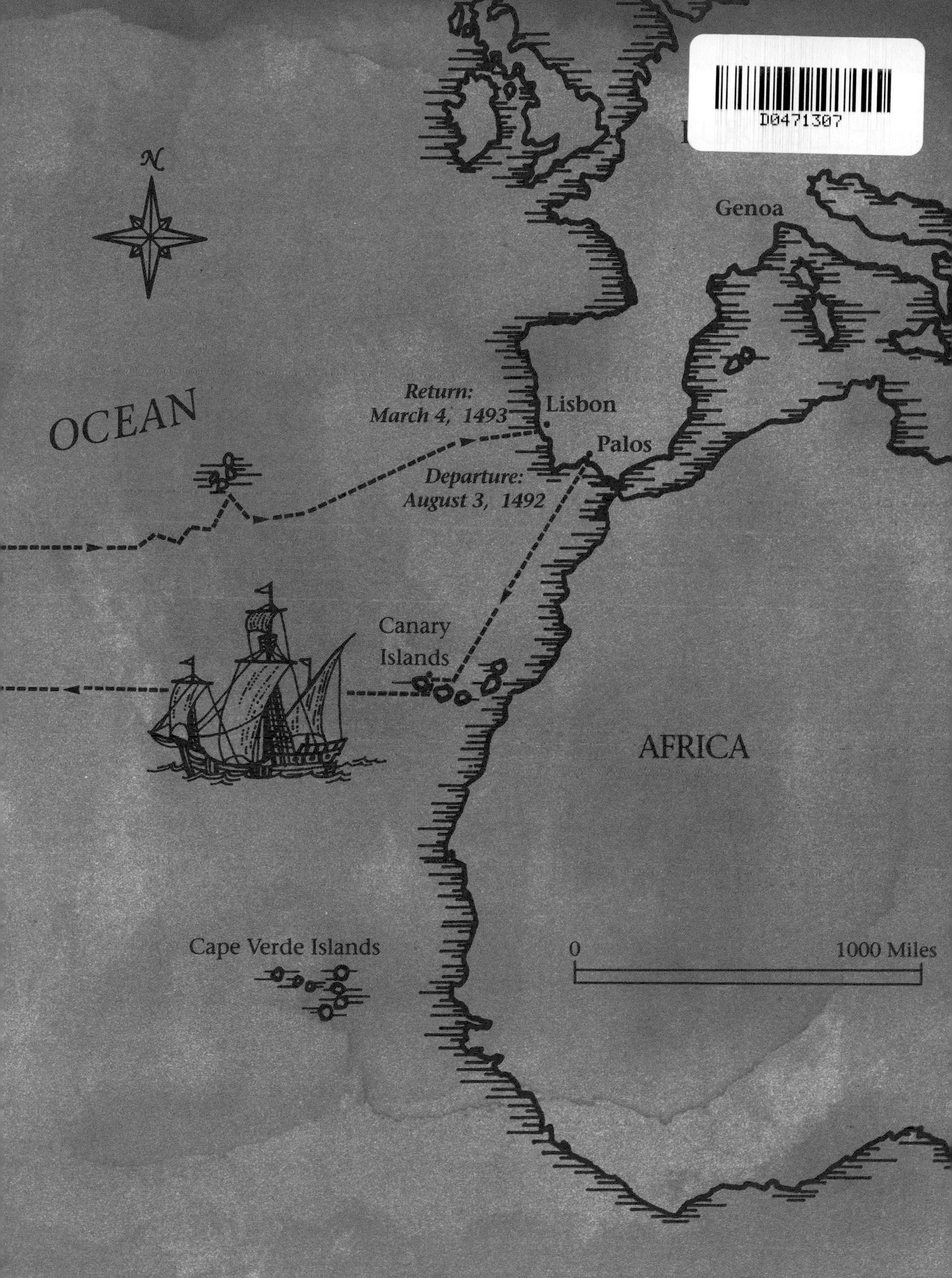

D0471307
N
OCEAN
Genoa
Return:
March 4, 1493
Lisbon
Palos
Departure:
August 3, 1492
Canary
Islands
AFRICA
Cape Verde Islands
0
1000 Miles

CHRISTOPHER COLUMBUS

HIS WORLD, HIS FAITH, HIS ADVENTURES

500th Anniversary Edition

His World, His Faith, His Adventures

Elaine Murray Stone

Illustrated by Pam E. Webb and Jeffrey Busch

Tyndale House Publishers, Inc.
Wheaton, Illinois

Library of Congress Cataloging-in-Publication Data

Stone, Elaine Murray, date
Christopher Columbus: his world, his faith, his adventures / Elaine Murray Stone; illustrated by Pam E. Webb and Jeffrey Busch.
p. cm.
Summary: A biography of Christopher Columbus, supplemented with historical and cultural information about the Renaissance world and the New World he explored.
"500th anniversary edition."
Includes bibliographical references.
ISBN 0-8423-0468-1
1. Columbus, Christopher—Juvenile literature. 2. Explorers—America—Biography—Juvenile literature. 3. Explorers—Spain—Biography—Juvenile literature. 4. Navigation—History—Juvenile literature. 5. America—Discovery and exploration—Spanish—Juvenile literature. [1. Columbus, Christopher. 2. Explorers.] I. Webb, Pam E. (Pam Elizabeth), date, ill. II. Busch, Jeffrey, date, ill. III. Title.
E111.S87 1991
970.01'5—dc20 90-71904

Library of Congress Catalog Card Number 90-71904
ISBN 0-8423-0468-1
Printed in Singapore

98 97 96 95 94 93 92 91
8 7 6 5 4 3 2 1

CONTENTS

Foreword

People worldwide have taken an interest in Christopher Columbus during the five hundredth anniversary of his discovery of America. But my involvement with Columbus goes back many decades.

In New York City, where I was born and raised, Columbus Day was celebrated each year with a huge parade down Fifth Avenue, where I lived. From an early age I was aware of places named in his honor, such as Columbus Circle and Columbia University.

But when I was in my teens, something happened that linked my life with his. My father, the late U.S. Ambassador H. Murray-Jacoby, was a close friend of General Raphael Trujillo, then president of the Dominican Republic. In 1937, Trujillo invited my parents to visit his country. While there, my father learned that the sarcophagus holding Columbus's remains was disintegrating. My father offered to donate a new metal resting place for the great explorer. In 1940, Trujillo erected a great lighthouse memorial to which Columbus's remains were transferred—in the casket given by my father.

Another connection with Columbus's history came in 1956 when my husband and I flew to Barcelona. A film had recently been made about Columbus, and the replica of the *Santa Maria* made for the film was floating in the harbor. We went on board the replica and were shocked at its small size. The flagship of Columbus's great venture offered terrible accommodations! The ceiling of the captain's cabin was so low we could not stand up, and Columbus was a very tall man. The crew had no place to sleep but on the deck. My admiration for Columbus soared as I marveled at his courage in sailing this small ship—and two others that were even smaller—into the unknown Atlantic.

A more recent involvement with the discoverer came through my daughter, Pam E. Webb, one of the illustrators of this book. Pam and her husband, Don, have lived on board a sailboat for the past six years in the Bahamas. Her main port has been Georgetown, Great Exuma, only a few miles from San Salvador and the second island Columbus visited. I have enjoyed cruising in the clear blue waters around those tropical islands, seeing with my own eyes the vistas first observed by Europeans in 1492.

My hope is that this book will make its readers more aware of Columbus, his four journeys to the New World, and his great contribution to history.

I want to thank the many people who helped me with the research, particularly Marian Griffin and Elfriede Raedler of the Eau Gallie Library and Rosemary Dyke of the Melbourne Library; Tyndale editor LaVonne Neff and designer Beth Sparkman; my editorial consultant, Julia Lee Dulfer; and my typist, Dana Pomeroy.

I dedicate this book to my grandchildren, David, Susan, and Lara Elaine Rayburn, with expectations that they, too, will make great discoveries to benefit mankind.

Elaine Murray Stone
Melbourne, Florida
October 1990

CHAPTER ONE

Christopher Columbus Prepares for Adventure

Genoa, a wealthy city

The city of Genoa had been wealthy for a long time. Over a thousand years before Columbus's day it prospered because its major port lay in the path of Phoenician, Roman, and Greek traders. During the Middle Ages, religious wars called the Crusades brought new commercial life into the city. Genoese traders hired out Genoa's merchant and galley ships to the Crusaders and lent money to eager borrowers. In Columbus's day the city was still wealthy, and its inhabitants were lovers of luxury.

When Christopher Columbus was born, over five centuries ago, life was very different from what we know today.

There was little freedom. Most places had no presidents and no elections. Kings and bishops ruled by divine right. The state told people what to do; the church told people what to believe. Those who disobeyed or disagreed were punished.

Most people were extremely poor. Lords and knights lived well. But serfs and peasants, who farmed the land, had little. Death was ever present. Plagues and other diseases, such as smallpox, wiped out entire populations. Many people died before the age of thirty.

And many children did not go to school.

But Christopher Columbus was luckier than most. He was born in Genoa, a city with a difference. Its ruler, the *Doge,* was elected by the people. The population was wealthy, for Genoa was a leader in trade and banking for much of Europe. And education was available for merchants' sons.

Genoese ships traveled east as far as Syrian and Byzantine ports. They returned with their holds bulging with silks, gold, and ivory. Even more profitable was their market in spices.

Christopher, the "Christ-bearer"

The name *Christopher,* which means "Christ-bearer," goes back to an ancient legend. There was once an ugly giant who made his living carrying people across a river. One day he was carrying a small child on his back. As they came to the center of the river, the child seemed to grow heavier and heavier. The giant feared they would both drown. The child then revealed that he was Christ, and the heaviness was caused by the weight of the world on his shoulders. The ugly giant took the name Christopher, and he became known as the patron saint of travelers. Christopher Columbus felt he must be a Christ-bearer, too, and carry the gospel of Christ to the heathen beyond the sea.

Not everybody in Genoa went to sea, of course. Many were skilled artisans. Columbus's parents, grandparents, and no doubt great-grandparents were weavers. In the fifteenth century, it was expected that children would learn their parents' trade.

The Columbus family did not expect their firstborn son to want to go to sea.

Born to Explore

Dominic Columbus and Susanna Fontanarossa were married in Genoa in 1445. They loomed woolen goods in their shop on the Via Mulcento, living in simple quarters above it. Susanna worked all day at her loom, pushing the heavy shuttle back and forth. Dominic marketed their fine woolen products in Genoa and smaller towns along the Ligurian coast.

It was five years before the couple conceived their first child. When he was a few days old, in 1451, they carried him to the nearby Church of St. Stephen. There he was baptized and named Christopher, meaning "Christ-bearer." Christopher's name and his faith would be important to him throughout his entire life.

Christopher was still a toddler when two events changed the course of history.

First, in 1453 the great city of Constantinople fell to Turkish invaders. Constantinople had been one of the world's great centers of classical learning and the Christian faith. Now Italy took the lead in art, literature, science, and philosophy. A rebirth, or *renaissance,* of culture was in full swing.

Second, in 1454 Johann Gutenberg of Mainz, in Germany, invented movable type, a fast new method of printing that made books much cheaper. Before, only the very wealthy could own books. Now everyone wanted to own books and learn to read.

Both events helped create an atmosphere of expectation and exploration. The time was ripe for Christopher Columbus.

Sea Dreams

When Christopher was seven years old, his father was appointed keeper of the Olivella Gate on Genoa's east side. Anyone entering or leaving the city by that gate had to pay a toll. With two incomes, Dominic could afford his oldest son's tuition.

Christopher was enrolled at the nearby school run by Franciscan friars. There he studied reading, writing, and drawing—no doubt very helpful to the future mapmaker. He was also an excellent Latin scholar, which pleased the friars.

After school Christopher was expected to help his parents in the shop. In those days a boy had to serve an apprenticeship in his father's craft and later join his guild. But Christopher hated working at the loom in his parents' hot, dusty workshop that reeked of wool. He much preferred the fresh salt air of Genoa's harbor.

There he watched the lumbering galleons, swift galleases, and long, slender galleys arrive from all parts of the Mediterranean. He loved listening to the seagulls' piercing cries above the breakwater. They seemed to call, "Come away! Come away!"

Christopher often talked to the many sailors hanging around the waterfront. He listened excitedly to their tales of faraway places and adventures at sea. Some told of harrowing shipwrecks; others, of pirate attacks or sea battles against their rival, Venice.

Christopher often walked home through the narrow cobblestone streets, dreaming of the time he would have such adventures. The woolen business was not for him. He could not escape to sea fast enough!

A Sea Change

For several years Dominic tried in vain to teach Christopher his trade. Gradually he came to realize that his son would never make a weaver. He was too restless. He spent too much time at the loom daydreaming. Perhaps he should be a sailor after all.

The Middle Ages

The thousand years from the fifth to the fifteenth centuries are called the *Middle Ages* or *Medieval* period. This was a time of knights and serfs, kings and warriors. During the Middle Ages, the Crusades were fought, great castles and cathedrals were built, and the Roman Catholic church became the greatest power in western Europe.

Latin, a common language

For fifteen hundred years, the people of Europe had a common language: Latin. Over the centuries Latin gradually changed into French, Spanish, Italian, Portuguese, and Romanian. Even so, educated people in Columbus's day still learned to write and speak Latin. It had become the language of scholars and of the church.

Genoa's sailors and merchants
Genoa was home to many expert shipbuilders and navigators. The city's energetic merchants established colonies in ports on the Aegean and Black seas. They went as far as Portugal and Castile, a kingdom of Spain. Through trading in the eastern Mediterranean, they brought home Asian silks, gold, and spices.

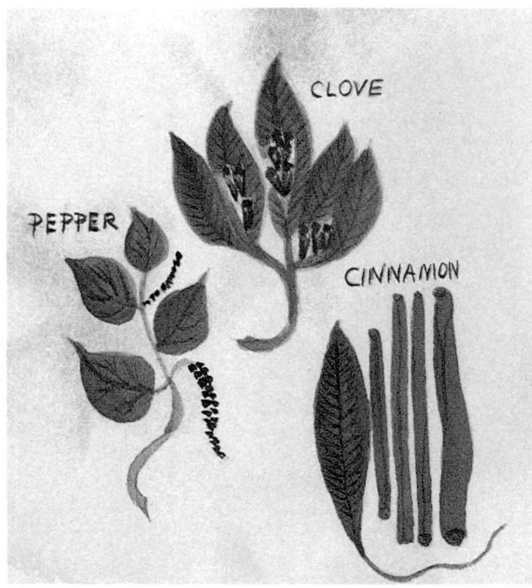

Spices
In Columbus's day there were no refrigerators to keep food from spoiling. Instead, salt and spices were used to preserve foods. Salt, used in curing meat, was fairly easy to obtain. But spices, used to make preserved meat taste good, were much harder to get. Spices came from the East Indies, thousands of miles from Italy. First they were brought to the Near East by caravan. Then they were shipped across the Mediterranean. By the time spices reached Genoese markets, they were very expensive.

Dominic found a way to help. For some time he had been selling his woolen goods along the Ligurian coast. When Christopher was fifteen, he was hired to help sail small merchant vessels to the nearby coastal towns. When the boats came to shore, Christopher sold his father's goods.

During the short voyages, Christopher would ply the captain with questions. How does the compass work? Why can't boats sail into the wind? What are the stars above us?

After one such trip, the weary captain had a talk with Dominic. "I think your son has a bent for the sea," he told Christopher's father. "He seems so interested in navigation. If he had some education in that science, I'm sure he could make an excellent pilot or navigator."

Dominic listened, but he did not know how to provide the training his son required. Then he learned about the University of Pavia, famous for its studies in naval science. It was only fifty miles north of Genoa. Dominic talked the matter over with Susanna. She said, "Our business is prospering. Tolls at the gate have increased. I think we can afford it."

So Christopher left home for Pavia. There he studied astronomy, geography, geometry, and navigation. At the university library he acquired a lifelong love of books, and he began saving money to buy some of his own.

His first purchase was Marco Polo's *Description of the World.* Christopher read that volume a hundred times, making notes in the margins and underlining passages that particularly intrigued him.

Escape from Pirates

The year he turned nineteen, Christopher was hired to pilot the *Roxanna,* a four-masted vessel under the command of Captain Gioffredo Spinola. It was headed for Chios, an island near Turkey. Chios was Genoa's last outpost in the eastern Mediterranean. It was completely surrounded by militant Muslims of the Ottoman Empire.

NAVIGATIONAL TOOLS OF THE 15TH CENTURY

A ship's speedometer

To measure the ship's speed, sailors used a *sandglass* and a *line and wedge.* First they tied knots every fifty-two feet along a long line of rope. Then they attached a triangular wedge of wood, held upright by a weight, to the line and threw it along the ship's side. As they threw the wedge over, they turned over the sandglass, a small hourglass filled with enough sand to last just thirty seconds. Speed was determined by the number of knots pulled through a sailor's hands every thirty seconds. If eight knots passed, the ship was said to be traveling eight knots. Each knot equaled one nautical mile per hour.

The Jacob's staff

The Jacob's staff, or cross staff, was a simple but inaccurate instrument invented in the thirteenth century. As its name implies, it was shaped like a cross. A navigator slid a crossbar back and forth on the the long section until the Polar Star was at the top and the horizon on the crossbar's lower end. The longbar, which had latitudinal numbers, gave the latitude in degrees, minutes, and seconds.

The lead line

A *lead line* was an instrument that measured the water's depth. It was marked off in fathoms (a fathom is six feet long), and it ended in a lead weight. This important tool protected ships from running aground or being destroyed by coral reefs. It was particularly useful to Columbus when he sailed through the shallow waters of the Bahamas. Ships today use electronic instruments to sound out these same shallow waters.

Portolanos

Portolanos were detailed charts of the coastline that guided ships safely into harbor. The locations of dangerous rocks, shoals, and sandbars were shown. Portolanos also noted tall trees, hills, capes, bays, mouths of rivers, lighthouses, and other important landmarks. Phoenicians first used portolanos thousands of years before Columbus. They were introduced to Europe by Prince Henry the Navigator.

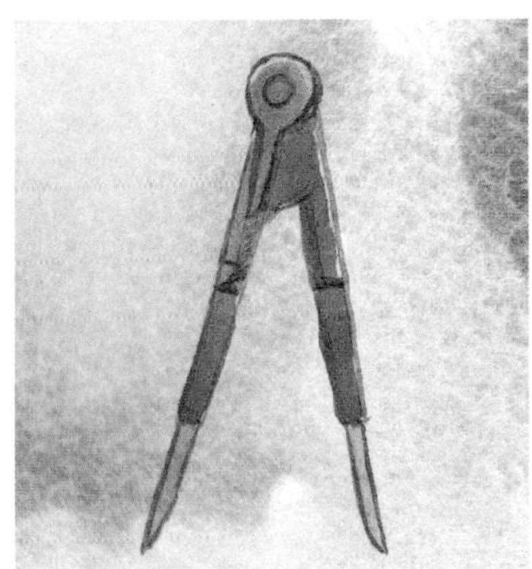

Dividers

A *divider* was a small metal instrument that measured distances on a chart. It was made of two spiked prongs joined together by a top hinge. The navigator used the sharp points to determine a distance on the chart. Then he held the divider in the same position on a graphic scale that gave latitudinal subdivisions. Navigators still use dividers today.

The Mediterranean Sea
The Mediterranean Sea was the major thoroughfare for the three continents bordering its shores: Europe, Africa, and Asia. Italians considered it their personal waterway, and two cities, Venice and Genoa, fought each other to rule it.

By this time Christopher had reached manhood. He was tall and well built, with steady blue-gray eyes. His complexion was fair but freckled, and he had thick red hair.

The *Roxanna* raised anchor and set sail around the foot of Italy to cross the Adriatic. It cruised through the calm blue Aegean Sea past the Greek islands.

One morning when Christopher was at the tiller, he sighted a strange vessel off the starboard bow. Calling to the sailor in the crow's nest, he asked, "What flag is that ship flying?"

"Blessed St. George!" exclaimed the terrified boy, "I think she's a Turkish pirate!"

A deckhand moaned, "We'll all be sold as slaves or put to the sword!"

But Christopher remained calm. Breathing a prayer for help, he commanded, "Lay on all canvas and prepare to alter course."

A dozen sailors scrambled up the rigging and let fly every inch of canvas. Others loaded the Lombards with powder and shot, sending a round of cannonballs across the pirates' bow. Then, taking advantage of the Turkish sailors' confusion, Christopher quickly outdistanced them.

Captain Spinola congratulated the young man for his quick action.

Galleys
Much of Genoa's trade was done using slave-propelled *galleys*. A galley was a long, narrow ship with one square sail. Slaves were chained to benches on each side and required to row the galley when the wind failed. Galleys worked well in Mediterranean waters, but failed in the heavy winds and waves of the Atlantic Ocean. Many chained slaves lost their lives at sea when the ships sank.

Escape to Chios

Two days later the Genoese ship reached Chios. Using navigational charts, Christopher guided the ship into the harbor.

Safely in port, Christopher was eager to row ashore and see the city. He climbed into the longboat and headed for town. He quickly discovered the streets of Chios cluttered with booths and street vendors. Men and women hawked their wares in many languages from stalls filled with exotic Eastern products.

His nostrils filled with the pungent smells of curry

from Ceylon, peppers from the East Indies, incense from Persia. Heavily veiled Arab women, perfumes wafting from their caftans, slipped mysteriously past.

Christopher was entranced with this city where East met West. When the *Roxanna* sailed for Genoa, he was not on board. There was too much to see and learn in Chios. He would stay and work as a wool merchant, but he would study the sea.

In Chios Christopher learned ancient navigational secrets of the Arabs: the Al-Kemal, astrolabe, and Joseph's staff. These devices, used by camel caravans taking goods through the trackless Arabian deserts, could just as well be used by sea captains, he thought.

He also learned that it took silks and spices three years to travel from the distant Orient to their destinations in Italy and France. *Isn't there a shorter way?* he wondered.

When Christopher had been in Chios about a year, the city was attacked and plundered by Turks. It was impossible to stay on this small island any longer. All foreigners had to leave immediately. Christopher volunteered to help sail the refugees home to Italy.

On the way he had much time to think. He wondered what would become of Genoa's rich trading connections in the East, now that the Turks were becoming more powerful. He wondered if he could find a better way to join East and West.

And he wondered what he would find waiting for him in Genoa.

Arab influence on exploration

The Spaniards and Portuguese were the greatest navigators and explorers of the fifteenth and sixteenth centuries, partly because Arabic culture flourished in Spain and Portugal. The Moors who conquered and occupied these countries for centuries treasured celestial navigation and mathematics.

The astrolabe

Geographers had used the astrolabe in a horizontal position for years. By holding it vertically, Martin Behaim adapted it for use at sea. He taught the pilots and navigators at Prince Henry's school how to use it as a navigational instrument. Columbus was never comfortable with the astrolabe. Perhaps he did not have enough mathematical knowledge to use it effectively.

CHAPTER TWO

Christopher Columbus Sees the World

The compass

Compasses were first used in ancient China, where they were considered a supernatural and secret treasure of royalty. The first Europeans to use the compass were from Columbus's hometown, Genoa. Mariners called the instrument the "Genoese needle." It contained a center needle magnetized by a lodestone cut from magnetite ore. Ships carried several lodestones for reactivating needles.

What makes a compass needle point north? The compass needle is suspended freely on a post. It points north when it is drawn by magnetic forces at the North Pole.

It was worse than Christopher had feared. Everything had changed in Genoa. His mother had died. His favorite brother, Bartholomew, had moved to Lisbon, Portugal—thirteen hundred miles away by ship. His father had started a wine business in Savona, about twenty miles up the coast from Genoa.

Christopher was worried. As the oldest son, he might be asked to take over the weaving shop. He hated weaving, and he hated running a shop. He would have to find work on a ship, and he would have to find it quickly.

Fighting Barbary Pirates

Luckily for him, a duke from southern Italy had lost a ship to Barbary pirates on the North African coast. The duke was too busy fighting with his neighbors to rescue it, however. He was happy to hire Christopher to sail to Tunis to free the *Fernandina.*

Although still a youth, Christopher was put in charge of the ship's older, more experienced crew. This pleased Christopher, but the sailors grumbled. They were afraid they would be captured by the cruel Tunisians.

Three days out to sea, the angry sailors revolted. They would not go with their young captain on this dangerous mission. What could Christopher do? He could not pos-

sibly overpower his entire crew—but he could trick them.

Christopher altered the ship's compass and pretended to head for Marseilles, a port in southern France. The sailors relaxed, and he continued sailing toward the African coast.

By the time the ship reached Tunis, the sailors had had a change of heart. Now they were eager to rescue the *Fernandina.* They fought hard, and they recaptured the valuable ship. This was a stunning victory for the young captain, who returned with all hands safe.

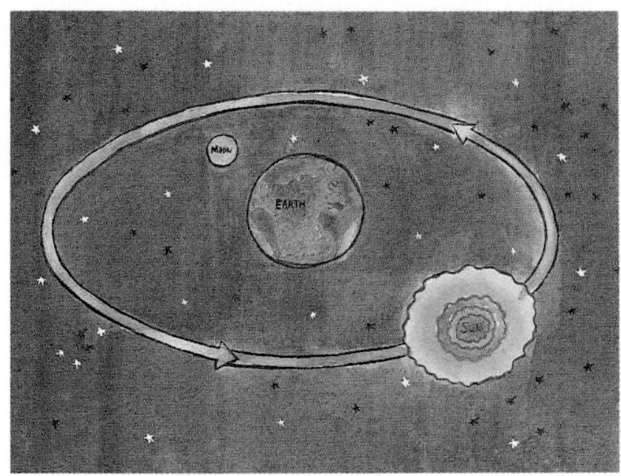

Which is at the center?
In Columbus's day, even the astronomers believed that the sun revolved around the earth. Half a century would pass before Copernicus would announce that actually the earth revolves around the sun. Still another generation would pass before Copernicus's idea was widely accepted.

Christopher Overboard

Back in Genoa, Columbus was praised for his success. He had no trouble finding his next job. This time he sailed with a fleet headed for the British Isles. He was pilot of one of the smaller merchant ships.

The fleet sailed west, past the mighty Rock of Gibraltar, into the ocean. For the first time Columbus viewed the vast expanse of the gray, brooding Atlantic. *Where does it end?* he wondered. *Do people live on the other side?*

The long column of ships was moving slowly off the coast of Portugal when a sailor spotted trouble ahead. Some French corsairs, or pirate ships, came into sight. The French began firing on the Genoese convoy.

Quickly the Italians loaded their guns, but the French ships fearlessly came alongside them. Soaking rags in pitch and setting them afire, the pirates launched their deadly missiles at the merchant ships.

Instantly the sails and rigging caught fire. Masts crashed to the decks as flames raced through the wooden vessels. Sailors, their clothes and hair on fire, jumped overboard. Last to leap into the sea was young Captain Columbus.

Travel dangers
Travel by land or sea was dangerous. Bandits lurked by the highways and robbed travelers. Sea travel was even more treacherous. Turkish and North African pirates preyed on all kinds of ships. Crews were sold into slavery and passengers were held for ransom. Then the pirates divided the ship's cargo among themselves. Because travel was so dangerous, many merchants desperately wanted to find a quicker, safer route to the East.

Clinging to a spar, Christopher began to swim through the choppy waves. Six miles later, the exhausted young man washed up on the Portuguese shore near the town of Lagos. Choking and coughing up salt water, Christopher began the sixty-mile walk to Lisbon, his brother's new home. How surprised Bartholomew would be to see him!

New Country, New Job

Christopher trudged into Lisbon owning nothing but the sun-dried clothes on his back. He did not know his way around the city, so he asked directions to Bartholomew's mapmaking shop.

"Bartholomew," Christopher called out as he knocked on the door. When Bartholomew came to the door, he didn't recognize the ragged figure.

"Don't you know me? I'm your brother, Christopher."

Bartholomew held his brother at arm's length and looked him over. "What happened to you?" he asked. "How did you get here?"

Christopher told him the whole story and then asked, "Don't you have a crust of bread for a starving man?"

Bartholomew apologized and went to the rear of the store to find some food. "You could do with a bath," he called over his shoulder.

After donning a clean outfit, Christopher looked around his brother's establishment. He saw drawing boards, dividers, rulers, and pens. Beside a new printing press were stacked sheets of paper for the maps. "Is business good?" Christopher asked.

"Not just good," said Bartholomew, "marvelous! This must be the best place on earth for a mapmaker to work. There is plenty of money for anybody connected with the sea."

Christopher began working in his brother's print shop. With the money he earned, he bought books to replace the ones he had lost in the shipboard fire.

Off and on for the next nine years, from 1475 to 1484, Christopher would live in Lisbon. Portugal was a good place for the young sea captain to learn more about his chosen lifework. The world's foremost school of navigation was in Sagres, not far from where Christopher came

Columbus's books

Christopher Columbus was an avid reader who treasured his book collection. He loved to make notes in the margins, and he took his books wherever he went. His favorite book topics were travel, mathematics, and astronomy. Columbus read Marco Polo's *Description of the World* at least a hundred times. Other favorites were Pliny's *Natural History of the World,* Pierre d'Ailly's *Imago Mundi* ("Picture of the World"), *The Story of Geography* by Pope Innocent II, and *The Travels of Sir John de Mandeville.*

Marco Polo

Marco Polo's adventures started when, at seventeen years old, he took a trip to China with his merchant father and uncle. After his return, Marco was captured during a battle at sea and imprisoned in Genoa. He used his three years in prison to record his fantastic experiences. As an adult, he continued to travel and to write. His book, *The Description of the World,* became an immediate success in handwritten copies. As printing developed, the book's popularity increased still more. In Italy his book became known as "The Milione" because of the money it earned from sales. It was Columbus's favorite book.

ashore. All through the fifteenth century Portuguese expeditions were discovering new lands and establishing colonies.

But even while learning about the sea, Christopher could not get rid of his desire to be at sea.

Sea Tales

Once, when business was slow, Christopher signed on with a ship headed for Iceland. He had never seen the North Sea, and the prospect fired his imagination.

The journey was difficult. Cruel winter storms battered the ship. The sun never shone. Immense swells lifted it, then dropped it. After days of constant battering, the ship put into Galway, Ireland, for repairs. An Irish pilot, experienced in navigating the North Sea waters, then joined the sailors.

During the long winter nights at sea, the men entertained each other with tales and legends.

A Welsh sailor told how one of their kings, Madoc, discovered an island far out in the ocean. He lived there with the natives the rest of his days.

Not to be outdone, a Scandinavian sailor boasted, "One of our princes, Leif Ericson, sailed across the top of the world to a far-off land. He took many of our people to settle there."

Then the Irish pilot told about Brendan, an Irish abbott who lived in the sixth century. Brendan wanted to go to the Promised Land of the Saints, believed to be far out in the western sea. He built a boat from oxhides sewn around a wooden frame. Taking some of his finest monks with him, Brendan headed west.

According to the legend, the sailors battled the sea for many weeks, finally arriving at an island where an angel met them. The angel addressed each of them by name. He gave them delicious fruits and precious gems. Then he said, "The Promised Land will only be made known to Brendan's successors in a time of great persecution of Christians."

Ulysses

The voyage of Ulysses, described by the Greek poet Homer in the *Odyssey,* is one of the oldest travel legends in the world. Ulysses' ten-year voyage included such adventures as fights with the one-eyed giant Cyclops and battles with strange sea monsters. This story was already over two thousand years old in Columbus's day—but voyagers still feared that, if they went too far, they might meet a sea monster!

Atlantis, the lost continent

The Greek philosopher Plato wrote a story about an island that sank west of Gibraltar and still rests beneath the sea. Explorers through the centuries have tried to find this island, called Atlantis.

When the swaying lamp was put out, Christopher thought about the tales he had heard. *What is really on the other side of the ocean?* he wondered.

Felipa

Columbus took the Brendan story seriously. *Hasn't Constantinople fallen to the Turks?* he asked himself. *Aren't Christians persecuted this very day by Muslims? Perhaps it is my destiny to discover the Promised Land!*

When Columbus returned home, he bought his own copy of *The Navigator,* Brendan's book about his voyage. He told Bartholomew about the many sailors in times past who had ventured west, even farther than the Portuguese had dared to go.

Bartholomew too had heard tales of islands in the sea. "Maybe we should rework our maps," he suggested.

But first, something important would happen to Christopher.

On his first Sunday home, Christopher attended church. Throughout the long service, his eyes frequently wandered to a beautiful young lady he had never seen before. When their eyes met, they both smiled shyly over folded hands.

Later Christopher learned her name. She was Felipa Perestrello e Moniz, and she was a student at the nearby convent school. She came from a titled family of the Azores, and her father had been governor of a newly discovered island.

Christopher began walking past the school every day, hoping for a chance to speak to Felipa. The day came when she noticed him, and soon the young couple fell madly in love. Felipa and the tall mariner were married the following year, 1479, in the convent chapel.

Felipa's widowed mother lived by herself on the island of Porto Santo, hundreds of miles west of Portugal off the African coast. Like most newlyweds, Christopher and Felipa were short of funds, so they moved into her mother's house.

St. Brendan

In the sixth century, Brendan, known as the patron saint of sailors, roamed the North Atlantic in a thirty-foot leather boat. His book, *Navigatio,* describes his landing on what may have been the shores of Newfoundland. In May of 1976 Tim Severin, a modern explorer, began to retrace Brendan's voyage. Using forty-nine oxhides prepared exactly as Brendan described in his book, he built a curragh similar to the saint's. In this seemingly fragile craft, Severin and his crew crossed the Atlantic, dodging ice floes and killer whales. In June of 1977 he landed at St. Johns, Newfoundland. Severin's successful journey makes Brendan's sixth-century account believable.

Vikings

Vikings, or sea warriors, were fierce sailors who journeyed for years at a time to distant fishing grounds. The Vikings, who came from the Scandinavian lands, plundered the coasts of England, France, and Scotland in their unique boats called longships. One such ship discovered in Denmark is seventy-six feet long and sixteen feet wide.

The Zeno map
A hundred years before Columbus, Nicolo Zeno, of Venice, was burned at the stake for claiming to have made a journey to North America along with his two brothers. Their map, carved on wood and printed in 1380, traces their journey.

The Hereford map
An ancient map that still exists today was created around 1400 by Richard de Haldingham and Henry de Lafford. Based on the travels of Sir John de Mandeville, it is drawn on parchment and displays brightly colored pictures of the world's marvels. Unlike previous charts, this map, known as the Hereford map, shows the world as round and the continents surrounded by oceans.

A circular map
Mapmaker Andria Bianco was kidnapped and forced into slavery on a Turkish galley. He managed to escape to Portugal at the height of Henry the Navigator's explorations. Everyone was astonished to hear about Bianco's travels and the navigational tricks he had learned from the Arabs. Bianco's circular map of the world is one of the most famous maps of his day. It depicts the land masses of Europe and Asia, shows castles and cathedrals, and pictures animals walking upside down below the equator.

Secrets and Old Maps

Porto Santo had been discovered only a generation before. The remote island fascinated Christopher. Many times after a rough winter storm, westerly winds washed strange objects ashore. Once Christopher found an unusual carved piece of a wood unknown to Europeans. Another storm brought lengths of bamboo.

Most astounding was the day two bodies washed up on the beach. Their skin color and features matched those of no race known to Christopher. He suspected they had been blown from islands far beyond the western horizon. What were those islands? How far away must they be?

In 1480 Christopher and Felipa's only son, Diego, was born. Not long afterward, Christopher found an old chest shoved into a corner at their house. Obviously no one had touched it for a long time.

"Felipa," asked Christopher, "what is in that battered old chest?"

Brushing off layers of dust, Felipa raised the lid. Christopher's eyes widened with surprise. His face flushed with excitement. "Look at this!" he exclaimed, pulling out yellowed charts, maps, and journals.

"Those must be from Grandfather's voyages," explained Felipa. "But that was so long ago. What good are they?"

To Christopher, they were immensely valuable. Examining the papers, he discovered page after page of navigational secrets known only to the Portuguese. He was amazed to find how far into the Atlantic their sailing ships, called *caravels,* had ventured.

One day Christopher sailed to the nearby island of Madeira. Browsing through a bookstore, he came upon twenty-three maps of the world, bound together by a string. Collected by Cardinal Philastre, a Frenchman famous for his study of geography, they were the finest maps he had ever seen. He bought them, aware that they could be his key to something great.

Tragedy Strikes

Not long after his return to Porto Santo, something terrible happened. Felipa got sick. There were no doctors on the island, and Christopher and her mother did not know how to help her. She grew weaker and weaker, and one night she died.

Christopher was heartbroken. He loved her dearly. And now what would become of Diego? Christopher was far from home. He had no home of his own, no income. He decided to pack his books and few belongings, take Diego, and sail for Lisbon.

Bartholomew welcomed his brother back. He set him to work in the print shop making paper. But working in a map shop was not to be Christopher's destiny.

One day Christopher learned that King Alfonso V was organizing an expedition down the west coast of Africa. Columbus applied for the job of *cartographer,* or mapmaker. He would map the unexplored area below Cape Bojador. Happily, he got the job.

Leaving Diego in Bartholomew's care, Christopher boarded one of the caravels waiting at anchor in the Tagus River, which meets the ocean at Lisbon.

The Underside of the Earth

As the small ships sailed into the open ocean, the crew began to share their fears. Rumors flowed about the underside of the world. People there walked upside down, it was said. The sea was so hot that ships' seams burst open. But Christopher was glad for the chance to find out for himself what the world was like below the equator.

Christopher enjoyed the cruise along the African coast. He took noonday sightings of the sun with the quadrant. He used dividers to make pricks on a chart to mark the ship's position and to show their route. He drew maps of the coastline, calculating the time changes as they moved west.

Contrary to the crew's fears, the sea did not boil. The

Pierre d'Ailly's map

French cardinal Pierre d'Ailly wrote *Imago Mundi* ("Picture of the World") in 1410, although it was not printed until 1480. This geography book encouraged Columbus in his planned venture to the Indies. D'Ailly's map was the first to place north at the top, and it was one of the first to portray a round world.

The antipodes

The word *antipodes* refers to places opposite each other on the globe. In Greek, it means "to have the feet opposite." Belief in the antipodes requires belief in a round world, and this caused a great stir in the church. Most religious men insisted the world was flat. They took the biblical image of the "four corners of the earth" literally. For believing in the antipodes, some people were denounced by the pope. A few were even burned at the stake!

air did not poison them. Instead, Africa was a pleasant land, with soft breezes and gently waving palm trees.

If men can travel this far south in the Atlantic, he reasoned, *they should be able to sail west as well. Perhaps I can do it myself. Perhaps I can find those islands beyond the horizon.*

But to achieve his dreams, he would need money—lots of it. And he didn't even have a regular job.

The caravel

In the fifteenth century, Prince Henry the Navigator of Portugal asked his shipbuilders to design a small, light ship for ocean voyages. They came up with the *caravel,* a small vessel—less than eighty feet long and weighing only a hundred tons—with high sides and three masts. The caravel was fast and easy to handle. All three of Columbus's ships were caravels.

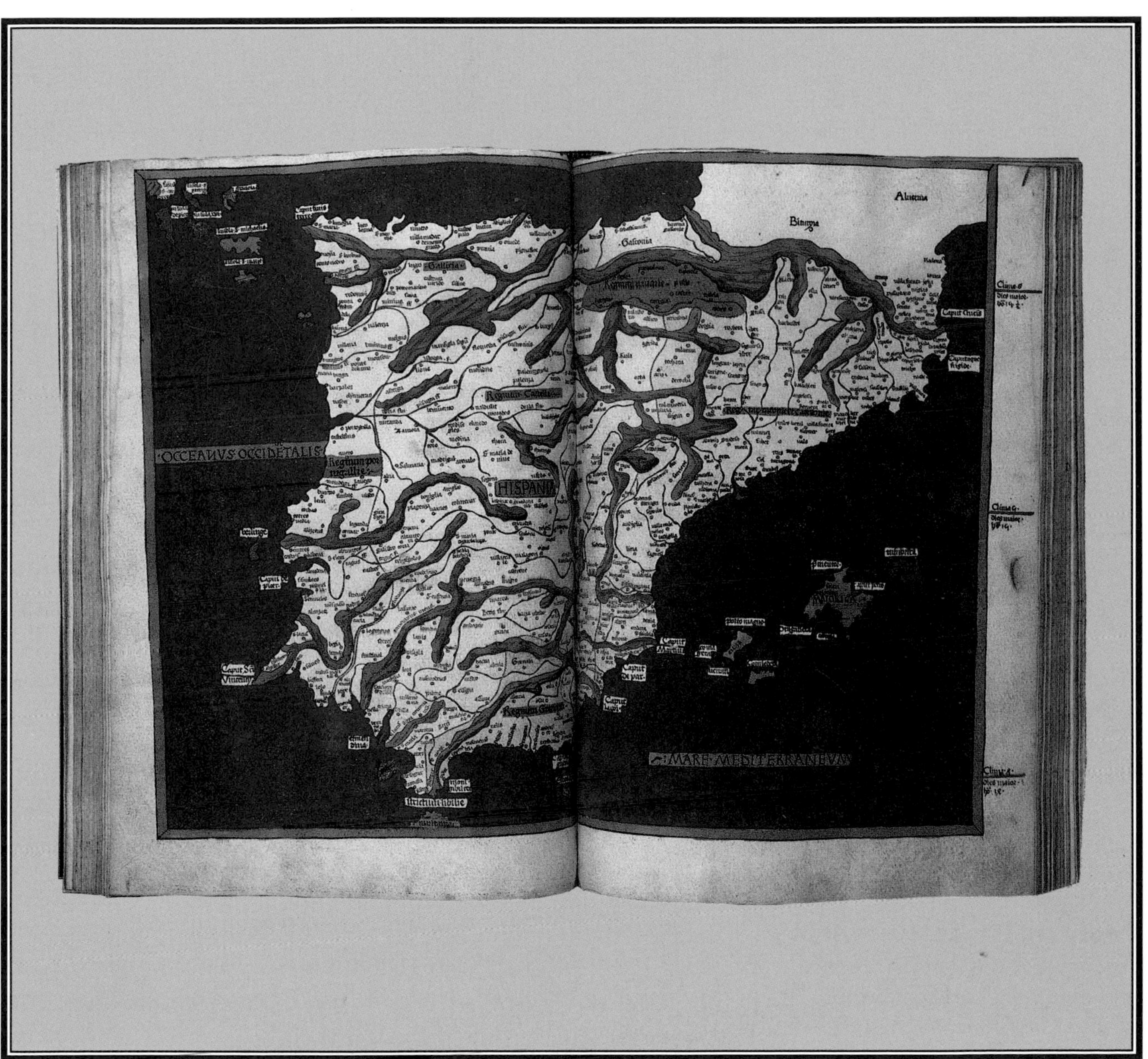

SPAIN, 1482.

This map of Spain was made just two years before Columbus moved there and began following Ferdinand and Isabella around the country.

CHAPTER THREE

Christopher Columbus Makes a Plan

After the voyage to Africa, Columbus returned to Lisbon. He began corresponding with Dr. Paolo Toscanelli, the world's top geographer.

One morning Christopher interrupted Bartholomew at the printing press. "Look!" he exclaimed. "Toscanelli has sent me a map!"

Bartholomew turned to see what all the excitement was about. "God has answered my prayers," Christopher almost shouted. He waved the large parchment in front of his brother. "It's just as he said in his letters. Europe and Asia cover most of the world. The Atlantic is no wider than our Mediterranean."

Bartholomew looked at the map and agreed.

"Do you realize what this means?" asked Christopher. "A good navigator with a sturdy caravel could cross the ocean in just a few days—and arrive at the islands of Japan!"

Bartholomew laughed. "You've been reading too much Marco Polo," he said. "Stop daydreaming and help me with this press."

Paolo de Pozze Toscanelli

Toscanelli was a famous scientist and mapmaker and contemporary of Columbus. In 1474 he wrote a letter to King Alfonso of Portugal: "Don't be surprised if I tell you that spices grow in the lands to the west, even though we usually say east. For he who travels east by land will always find the same lands in the west." Columbus corresponded with Toscanelli about this. Arriving at the same conclusion, he determined to do something about it.

The Narrow Atlantic Ocean

Christopher turned the heavy screw, but his head was full of visions of the palace of Kublai Khan. How wonder-

BUSCH

Kublai Khan

Kublai Khan was the Mongol emperor during part of the thirteenth century, when Marco Polo made his voyage. The Mongol Empire was huge: it included most of today's China, Soviet Union, and Eastern Europe. Columbus hoped to find Kublai Khan's empire by sailing west, but two problems prevented this. First, the entire continent of North America stood in his way. Second, the Mongols were no longer in power. Without modern communications media, he had no way of knowing that the Ming Dynasty was now in power.

Esdras

The Book of Esdras in the Apocrypha (included in some editions of the Bible) claimed that the earth was covered by six parts land and one part water. Actually, water covers over 70 percent of the earth's surface.

ful to walk through its hundreds of rooms and return with chests bursting with treasures! With Toscanelli's map, such a voyage looked possible. All he needed now was someone to finance it.

His plan began to take shape. One morning as he read his daily Bible passage, Columbus came across this verse from the Book of Esdras, part of the Apocrypha: "God created the world in seven parts, six of them dry land and the seventh water" (2 Esdras 6:42).

To Columbus, this quotation was conclusive. The area from Lisbon on the west to Japan on the east made up the six parts of land. The Atlantic ocean obviously represented the seventh part.

Columbus knew that, according to Ptolemy, the earth's circumference at the equator was eighteen thousand miles. One seventh of eighteen thousand is less than twenty-six hundred. A ship can average one hundred miles a day. Therefore, Columbus figured, he could reach Japan in thirty days or less. Why not try it?

He decided to approach King John II of Portugal to ask his help. John claimed to be as interested in exploration as his famous great-uncle, Henry the Navigator. He was already plotting new ways to reach the rich spices of the East Indies, now that the Mediterranean was controlled by the Turks.

Christopher requested an audience with the king.

Going East by Going West

On the appointed day, he arrived at court in a new suit of clothes. The unknown mariner stood before the king and addressed him boldly.

"Your Majesty," he said, "I have completed the charts King Alfonso commissioned of the west coast of Africa." He handed the carefully drawn maps to an aide.

"But sir," he continued, "at sea I conceived a plan that is far more important than these charts. This plan could make Portugal the wealthiest nation on earth."

"What might that be, Captain Columbus?" asked the

bored king, yawning into his lace handkerchief.

"Sire, it is not necessary to send your ships on a long, dangerous journey around Africa to reach the Indies. I know how to do it in less than a month."

The king leaned forward, suddenly taking notice.

"I can reach the Indies by sailing a ship west across the Atlantic Ocean. The way west is shorter and faster."

The king threw back his head and roared with laughter. "The African sun has made you mad!" he said. "Go back to your maps and charts. I have no time for fools."

Christopher's face fell. His shoulders drooped as he backed out of the king's presence. He trudged slowly home, the king's laughter ringing in his ears.

"I have been cruelly humiliated before the entire court," Christopher told his brother. "The king refused even to consider my venture. He laughed, Bartholomew. He laughed. What am I to do?"

"Sit down and let's talk about it," said Bartholomew. "With God's help, we will find a way."

Bartholomew's Globe

The brothers talked until dusk. Bartholomew rose to light the lamp. He returned with a large, round object.

"While you were at sea," he said, "I devised a better method to display a map. See, I have cut the map in sections and then glued them to a sphere. I call this my globe of the world."

Christopher examined the globe, turning it this way and that.

"With my globe you can show how you plan to cross the ocean. People will see that your route is shorter than any other."

"This is marvelous!" said Columbus, feeling better already.

"Why not show this globe to another king?" Bartholomew suggested. "When the Venetians showed no interest in Giovanni Gabatto, he moved to England to work for King Henry. He has even changed his name to John

A magnificent palace
Columbus was intrigued by Marco Polo's description of Kublai Khan's unusual palace. "The palace of the Great Khan covers six square miles and consists of four hundred rooms. Rooms and halls are covered with sheets of gold, silver, and blue-glazed tile. Lions and dragons are carved from wood as decoration," Polo wrote. "The roof is made of silver and gold; the ceiling carved and painted with gold. The hall is so great that six thousand guests can be served dinner at one time."

Franciscan friars
Who were the Franciscan friars? The word *friar* means "brother," and the Franciscan friars were religious men (monks) who lived as brothers in a community founded by Francis of Assisi. St. Francis, who lived three hundred years before Columbus's time, believed God's followers should lead humble and gentle lives. Franciscan friars gave Columbus spiritual support. Today, five hundred years later, Franciscans are still active around the world.

Cabot. You might ask Henry, or perhaps Ferdinand of Aragon."

Christopher sat deep in thought. He had already moved too many times. "Not another change for little Diego," he moaned.

But Bartholomew continued, "Spain is strong and rich. I say go to Spain and ask Ferdinand for help."

"After the sorry reception King John gave my plan," said Christopher, "I owe no further allegiance to Portugal. Perhaps I will go to Spain."

"And I can close the shop and try my luck in England," offered his brother. "The English are expanding their navy and exploring new lands. I will take my globe and explain your plan to Henry. Cheer up, Christopher. We are on our way to fame!"

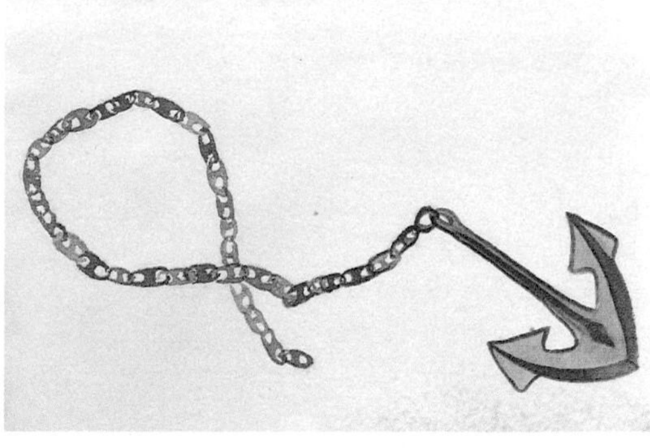

Anchors
Primitive anchors were made by tying a heavy stone at the end of a rope. By Greek and Roman times, iron anchors were used. In Columbus's day, Spanish and Portuguese ships carried a one-thousand pound iron anchor with an iron-link chain at the ship's bow and two smaller anchors at the stern. Most shipwrecks occurred when the anchors failed to hook securely. The anchor became a Christian symbol: we are safe only when Christ is our anchor.

Columbus in Spain

Taking Diego with him, Christopher left Lisbon at night. His destination was Palos, on the coast of Spain. He would ask the Spanish king and queen for assistance and funds for his venture.

At Palos Christopher learned of a nearby Franciscan monastery, La Rábida, where the kindly friars would care for Diego. Saying good-bye to the small boy, Christopher set out for Córdova to see King Ferdinand and Queen Isabella.

For centuries Spain had been a collection of small kingdoms dominated by the Moors, Muslim immigrants from North Africa. Ferdinand of Aragon desperately wanted to chase out the Moors. Isabella of Castile had the same dream. Ferdinand and Isabella each held huge parcels of land. When they married, in 1469, a large part of Spain was unified.

Ferdinand and Isabella were in Córdova getting ready for battle against the Moorish king when Columbus arrived there. They had driven the Moors out of all parts of Spain except Granada, about fifty miles away. For the time being, they were too busy with battle plans to listen to Columbus.

Christopher knew he had a long wait ahead of him. He found simple lodgings at an inn run by Enrique de Harana and his beautiful daughter, Beatrice.

Christopher had little to do but think about his planned voyage to the Indies. He ached to share his thoughts with someone. The lonely widower and the innkeeper's daughter soon became fast friends. After she finished her daily chores, the two talked long hours about his dream.

Beatrice

"What do you plan to tell the king when you finally see him?" Beatrice asked.

"I'll say a ship can reach the Indies by sailing west across the ocean. God has told me that this route is possible."

"But wouldn't you be afraid of sea monsters, or of dropping off the edge of the earth? Who would sign on for such a voyage?" she asked.

"Beatrice, that is only fantasy. I have sailed south and north, east and west. Never have I seen anything out of the ordinary, except whales and sharks. Those tales you have heard come from Sir John de Mandeville. I have a copy of his book. What a great imagination!"

"You mean the world isn't flat?" asked Beatrice.

"Of course not," he answered. "Mariners have known the world is round for years. At sea, it is easy to tell. When another ship approaches, first its mast appears and then gradually the entire ship, as if it were coming uphill. The world has to be round."

"But Christopher, no one has ever crossed the ocean before. It is an endless journey. I would fear for you."

Columbus shook his head. "Others have done so already. Brendan. Leif Ericson. Even a group of Portuguese.

Education and faith

Columbus wrote to Ferdinand and Isabella: "From a very young age I began to follow the sea and have continued to this day. The art of navigation incites those who pursue it to enquire into the secrets of the world. I have had dealings and conversations with learned men, priests and laymen, Latins and Greeks, Jews and Moors, and many other sects. I have made it my business to read all that has been written on geography, history, philosophy, and other sciences. This our Lord revealed to me, that it was feasible to sail from here to the Indies, and placed in me a burning desire to carry out this plan."

A spherical map

Joannes de Sacrubusco, a thirteenth-century astronomer at the University of Paris, was the first to draw a spherical map.

Córdova

Córdova was famous in the fifteenth century for its thirteen-thousand weavers and fine leatherworkers. It is still known for the fine leather called *Córdovan,* originally made from goatskin but now usually made of horsehide.

I must find out for myself. Have faith in me, Beatrice. I need your trust."

His statement made Beatrice realize what she had long suspected. Their friendship had turned into deep love. Even if all others scoffed at Christopher, she would believe in him and his dream.

A Meeting with Isabella

In May 1486, after waiting for two years, Christopher finally received the royal command to appear at court. However, it was not to speak with the king. His audience would be with Queen Isabella.

Beatrice brushed off Christopher's faded clothes as best she could, then kissed him good-bye as he set off for the palace. He carried his charts and globe with him.

Columbus bowed deeply before the queen. He noted her fine features and thick auburn hair. Isabella, in turn, was impressed with the tall captain's good looks and charm. She listened patiently to his presentation. But his mathematical explanations and navigational terms were beyond her understanding.

The queen sighed. "My dear Columbus, I find this matter most difficult. I cannot come to an immediate decision. I prefer that you present these same facts and figures to scholars better prepared to make sense of them."

Christopher was shocked. He had waited for such a long time! But the queen continued, "I shall have my adviser, Father Talavera, set up a commission to study your project. He can call together astronomers, navigators, and cosmographers. We can all meet again at Christmas."

Although deeply disappointed, Columbus thanked her graciously. "May God bless you and your family," he added.

"I would that you also be blessed," said Isabella. "I hereby order our court almoner to provide you with twelve thousand maravedís a year for your support."

Two million maravedís
In 1486, the Spanish court awarded Columbus a yearly fee of twelve thousand maravedís so that he would not ask another court to finance his voyage. The eventual cost of the voyage was 2 million maravedís. The ancient maravedi was a gold coin, but these were copper coins of much less value.

Henry the Navigator
Young Prince Henry of Portugal became interested in Africa after accompanying his royal father on a battle expedition to North Africa. From stories he heard, he realized Portugal could make important discoveries in Africa's interior. Henry set up the famous "Sagres" school at the westernmost point in Portugal. Great cosmographers, astronomers, and mathematicians from Europe and the Middle East attended. Ambitious Prince Henry even resurrected Ptolemy's maps and writings from A.D. 150 for his navigators to use.

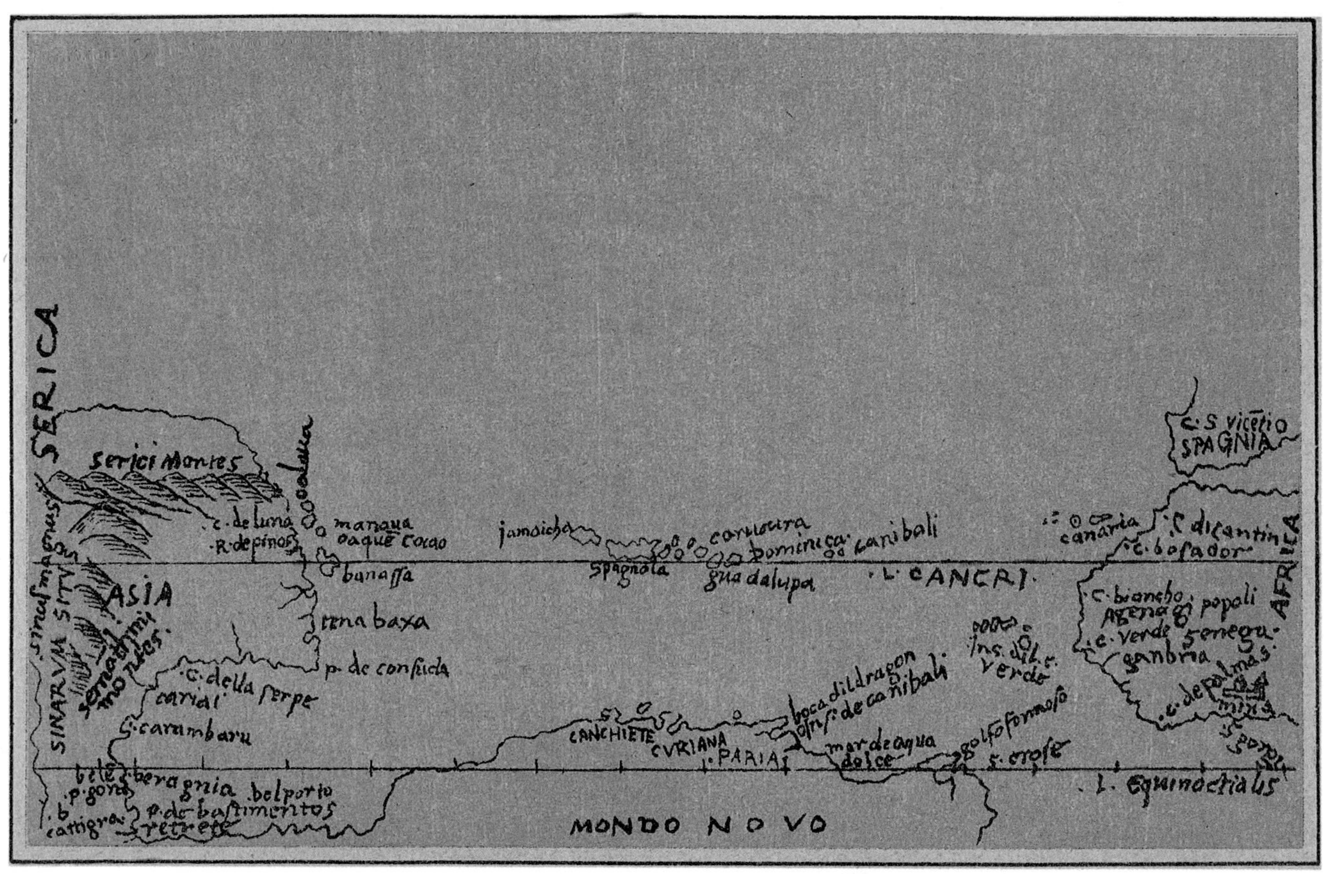

Bartholomew Columbus drew this map of the New World. It shows that he did not know a new continent lay beyond the Caribbean islands: the western continent is Asia!

Gold and pearls
Marco Polo described Cipangu, known as Japan today, as a place where gold abounded. "Gold is mined there beyond measure," he wrote. "The great ruler of Cipangu has a palace entirely covered with gold. The floors and pavements are of pure gold. All the halls and windows are adorned with gold. The roof is made of golden tiles two fingers thick. . . . Pearls are abundant in this land. Everyone is buried with a great pearl in his mouth. They have so many precious stones that no one could count the riches of it."

Columbus the bookseller
In 1476 three German brothers named Müller set up a printing press in Córdova. While Columbus was waiting for Queen Isabella to approve his first voyage, he worked for the Müllers as a bookseller.

Christopher could hardly believe his ears. Though plans for the voyage were delayed, at least he could now properly care for himself, Beatrice, and Diego. Suddenly life had taken a turn for the better! He almost danced all the way home.

A Meeting with the Scholars

But the Christmas meeting was a disaster. Christopher met all week with the experts gathered by Father Talavera. They questioned him relentlessly. No one seemed to understand.

"On what do you base your assumption that the Atlantic Ocean is narrow enough to be crossed?" asked a famous geographer.

Another asked, "How can you be certain that the islands of Japan lie on the other side? What makes you think you can find them?"

A third observed, "I don't believe the ocean is navigable. Our ships and men will be lost."

"I assure you that none of what you claim is possible," said a bent, old priest, stroking his beard. "The church has never written of such a route. It cannot be done."

But Columbus was not ready to give up. He quoted Toscanelli and showed his map. He referred to Marco Polo's writings and showed his globe. He explained every reason for his belief and every detail of his plan.

When this did not work, he tried a different approach. "Think of the fortune in gold and spices such a trip could bring to Spain. Think of how the world will view Spain. We all will be heroes."

The scholars shook their heads in disbelief. "Where does this fool get such ideas?" they clucked to one another. The council was adjourned, and Columbus was sent on his way.

In their report, issued four years later in 1490, the scholars said, "The committee judges that the claims and promises of Captain Columbus are vain and worthy of rejection. . . . The Western Sea is infinite and unnavigable. The Antipodes are not livable, and his ideas are impracticable."

Ignored Again

Columbus spent the six years from 1486 to 1492 following Ferdinand and Isabella as they moved their court from place to place. At a moment's notice he was ready to present charts, maps, facts, and figures. But the king and queen were always too busy with battles. They had no time, money, or energy to give to the determined Italian sea captain.

During that time of wandering, in 1488, Christopher and Beatrice had a son. They named him Fernando after the king Christopher so much wanted to see.

The year 1492 was only two days old when the Moors finally surrendered Granada, their last foothold in Spain. Columbus joined in the triumphant procession to the Alhambra, the castle of the Moorish king. Circling up the winding roads to the city walls, the happy Spaniards entered the fallen city with trumpets playing and banners flying. King Ferdinand rode in on a white steed. The endless battles were over. Spain was united and at peace.

As he entered the city, Columbus thought, *At last the king and queen will have time to listen to me.* But still he was not called.

The long-awaited moment came at last in late January. Isabella, seeing Columbus's shabby clothes, granted him a mule to ride and a purse of gold ducats to purchase clothes proper for a courtier. But once again she offered no money to support his trip west to the Indies.

Columbus returned home, deeply depressed.

Fernando

Columbus's son Fernando was born in 1488. At age thirteen, he accompanied his father on his fourth voyage. He later accompanied his brother and uncle to the New World and helped establish churches and monasteries there. Fernando was wealthy enough to be a student and book collector. His library included 15,370 books!

What Columbus was like

Washington Irving, the American nineteenth-century novelist, described Columbus as a scholar, a visionary, practical, self-disciplined, liable to powerful impulses, forgiving of others, free of revenge, having great skill in managing others. Columbus also was conspicuous for his great height and commanding appearance.

CHAPTER FOUR

Christopher Columbus Gets Ready to Go

The Columbus family's religion

It is believed that Christopher's great-grandfather fled from Catalonia, Spain, in 1371 during a pogrom against the Jews. He settled in Genoa, which was more tolerant than many other cities. At that time he changed his name from Colón to Colombo and became a Christian.

The strain of waiting had aged Columbus. He was only forty years old, but his hair had turned white. It hurt him that no one believed his plan would work. Kings, scholars, and courtiers made fun of him. Some even laughed in his face.

Columbus decided to visit the peaceful Franciscan monastery at La Rábida, the place he had left Diego seven years earlier. Although Diego had left the monastery school in 1491, it still seemed a good place to visit.

At the monastery, Christopher knew, he could unburden his heavy heart to the kindly friars. They would pray for him and counsel him.

Going for Help

After riding on his mule for several days, Columbus crossed the bridge to La Rábida and dismounted in the shadow of the monastery. He banged on the wooden gate.

Eventually an old friar made his way to the entrance. Tugging at the heavy door, he cried, "Welcome, Captain Columbus! Come in! I will tell Father Juan that you are here."

"Do not disturb the prior if he is at prayers," whispered Columbus.

Called by God

"Who shall go over the sea for us and bring the word unto us, that we may hear it and do it?" This biblical quotation from Deuteronomy 30:13 inspired Columbus to venture to the Far East so that he could bring the gospel to the heathen.

Eratosthenes

Three centuries before Christ, Eratosthenes found a way to measure the earth. His calculation of the earth's circumference at twenty-nine thousand miles was wrong by only five thousand miles. The earth's circumference is actually just over twenty-four thousand miles. In his seven volumes on geography, Eratosthenes used mathematics and divided the globe into zones, parallels, and meridians.

Ptolemy

The Greek mathematician Ptolemy was the highest authority on world geography for over a thousand years, from the second century A.D. up to Columbus's time. Also considered the founder of trigonometry, he discovered how to represent the earth's latitude and longitude on flat paper. Ptolemy's demonstration of a round world convinced Columbus he could sail west and arrive in the East Indies. Ptolemy's error in calculating the earth's circumference at eighteen thousand miles also contributed to Columbus's first transatlantic journey. He thought the trip would be shorter!

"You can talk," said the little friar. "Chapel is over, and Father Juan is in his study. Follow me."

Columbus strode after the old man, who tripped on his long robe in excitement. "And how is Master Diego?" he asked. "Will he be coming back here for his schooling?"

"Diego is fine," said Columbus. "He will come back to you soon."

The friar paused before a closed door and knocked. "Enter," echoed a deep voice. As Columbus pushed the door open, the prior came forward to greet him. "Dear friend," he asked, "what brings you so far from court?"

Columbus's face reddened. Hurt and embarrassed, he found his situation hard to talk about. Father Juan saw his discomfort. He said, "Perhaps it will be easier to talk if we walk around the garden."

"As you wish, Father," replied the downcast man.

The prior led the way to the cloister surrounding the monastery garden. As the two men strolled along the covered walk, he waited for Columbus to begin. Finally Father Juan asked, "My son, what is troubling your soul?"

Hesitantly, Columbus began.

Waiting in Faith

"As you know from our talks and letters," he said, "I have followed the teachings of Ptolemy. He said that the earth is not flat. It is a sphere, eighteen thousand miles in circumference.

"Many church leaders disagree with this explanation. They have poisoned the court against my efforts to seek a route to the Orient by sailing west."

The prior nodded sadly, and Columbus continued.

"Based on the knowledge I have gained from my studies, along with my own observations of winds and currents, I am convinced that with a few good ships I can find a faster route to the riches of the East."

"What you say makes sense to me," said the prior. "But some people are hard to persuade. Come, let us rest awhile on this bench. My old bones ache and my muscles have lost their strength. You, though, are still a young man. You must not let anything hold you from your destiny."

Columbus sighed heavily. "What can I do?" he asked sadly. "Everyone tells King Ferdinand that my plan will end in failure and death. The king's advisers tell him to have nothing to do with my expedition. Where can I turn?"

"My son," said the prior, "the Lord who created the universe knows your intention is pure and your plan is based on logic. Have faith in yourself, and in God. And stay with us at La Rábida until the court decides. Here you will find peace and support."

A Mission from God

Columbus remained at the monastery several days. One day a royal messenger galloped up to its entrance. In his pouch was a letter from Ferdinand and Isabella. Pounding on the gate, he shouted, "Open in the name of the king!"

When he reached the mariner, he cried out, "Good news, Captain Columbus! The king is ready to back your expedition to the Indies. You must return at once."

Columbus tore open the letter. His face broke into a huge smile. "At last!" he exclaimed. "Thank God!" Ready to leave immediately, he asked only for a few minutes to bid farewell to the friars.

The prior placed a firm hand on Columbus's shoulders. "My son," he said, "never forget that you are the Christ-bearer. You will reach the Indies. It is your destiny to bring the gospel of Christ to the heathen in those lands."

"Yes, Father," said Columbus, "the gospel is a gift I will take to those who dwell in darkness outside our Christian faith."

Striking his whip against a column, the impatient messenger mumbled, "It is time to leave." But Father Juan held Christopher back.

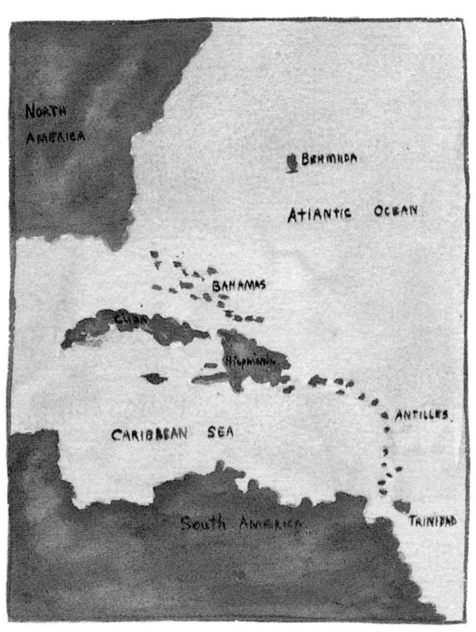

The New World

The term *New World* was coined by Peter Martyr, who wrote thirty-seven volumes on discoveries in the Western Hemisphere. Although he never visited the New World himself, his writings, which describe Columbus's discoveries, are still used by scholars. Martyr met Columbus in Spain during his triumphant return from the New World.

The Crusades

During the eleventh, twelfth, and thirteenth centuries, Europeans launched numerous military expeditions to free Jerusalem from the Saracens, who ruled the Holy City. These religious wars are called the *Crusades*. They did not accomplish their aim. In Columbus's lifetime, the holy places were still under Muslim control. It was his great dream to free them. He vowed to use a part of his wealth from the New World to accomplish this.

Prior Juan Pérez

Prior Pérez of La Rábida monastery personally visited Queen Isabella of Spain to ask her help in financing Columbus's voyage. Prior Pérez had been her confessor, or personal pastor, and he could arrange a royal visit on any occasion.

An alternate port

In 1492, when Columbus was ready to sail, he had to use the port of Palos and not the much larger port of Cádiz. The Spanish Inquisition had begun, and the king had signed a proclamation expelling all Jews from Spain. Over ten thousand Jewish refugees were assembled in Cádiz awaiting space on ships that would transport them to Holland, England, and other welcoming countries. Cádiz was used entirely for refugee ships.

"Do you expect to return from the Indies with great riches?" he asked.

"Oh yes," said Christopher. "Ivory, silks, caskets of gold and pearls. We will return with much treasure, I assure you."

"In that case," said the prior, "I beg you to give some to free the Holy Sepulcher in Jerusalem."

"Certainly, Father," promised Columbus. "I pledge a tenth of all the treasure we discover. It shall be used to raise an army to free Jerusalem from unbelievers."

"That is what I expected," said the satisfied prior. "And now let me give you my blessing."

Columbus knelt to receive it. Then, his heart overflowing, he mounted his mule and left with the messenger for the court of Ferdinand and Isabella.

Lord Admiral of the Ocean Seas

This time Columbus was not kept waiting. He was ushered at once into the royal presence. The date was April 17, 1492.

Queen Isabella greeted him warmly. "At last we have expelled the infidels from our land," she said. "Now we can turn our thoughts toward other matters."

"Yes, Your Majesty," agreed Columbus, waiting to hear the important news.

"As you already know," the queen continued, "the Portuguese have long been leaders in exploration. It is time for Spain to make discoveries of our own. Unfortunately, our coffers have been emptied by war. But there is still a way to finance your enterprise. I pledge my personal jewels to sponsor your attempt to discover a new route to the Indies."

Columbus could not believe his eyes as the queen unclasped ropes of pearls from around her neck. Then she worked the heavy gold rings, ablaze with diamonds and rubies, from her slender fingers.

"Here, Admiral Columbus," she said, "take these jewels and make good use of them for the honor of Spain."

"Thank you, Most Gracious Majesty," said Columbus, humbled by her generosity. "But did I hear you say *admiral?"*

"Yes," replied Isabella, smiling. "I appoint you Lord Admiral of the Ocean Seas and viceroy of all lands you discover. You will have the hereditary title of *Don."*

Columbus kissed the monarch's hand. "Your Majesty, I shall bring you chests brimming with even greater treasure than you have given me today. You are the most gracious of queens."

Then the new admiral bowed his way backward out of the throne room, grinning all the way to the door.

Getting Ready

The admiral had little time to reflect on his new title. There was so much to do to prepare for his voyage.

Before leaving Córdova for Palos, his port of embarkation, he said good-bye to Beatrice and Fernando. In May he returned Diego to the school at La Rábida, as he had promised, and said farewell to the friars. Only then did he begin to look for ships, provisions, and a crew.

In Palos lived three brothers named Pinzón. Like Columbus, they had sailed to many distant places. Unlike him, they were rich. In fact, they owned several ships.

With the money raised by the queen's jewels, Columbus bought from them a sturdy one-hundred-ton boat, naming it the *Santa María* in honor of the mother of Jesus. The town of Palos then gave him two small caravels named the *Niña* and the *Pinta.*

He put the *Niña,* a small boat of fifty tons, under the command of Vicente Pinzón. He made Martín Alonso Pinzón captain and Francisco Pinzón pilot of the *Pinta,* a similar boat.

The admiral then combed Palos for a crew. However, no one wanted to sign on for such a foolish venture. Most were certain that no one who sailed with Columbus would ever be seen again.

In the end, the admiral went to the local jail, which

Sails

Fifteenth-century ships were faster and easier to handle than earlier ships. One reason was improved design of the sails. The earliest sails, used on Nile River boats in Egypt, were triangular. Viking ships used square sails. Columbus's ships used both types of sails. The foremast and mainmast had square sails, and the mizzen had a triangular sail.

was full of sailors locked up for bad debts or for brawling in the dockside taverns. "How many of you are experienced seamen?" he asked. Most of the prisoners raised their hands.

"All who sign on for my voyage to the Indies will be pardoned and released," Columbus told them.

A shout of "Hurrah!" rose through the crowded jail. Men rushed to offer their services. Columbus was happy; his crew was complete.

Bill of lading: second voyage

For his second voyage, Columbus requested salt meat, wheat flour, wine, oil, vinegar, sugar, molasses, rice, almonds, raisins, and honey. He also asked for carpenters, axmen, masons, and ditchdiggers to build a fort and city, as well as miners to dig for gold.

Setting Sail

Palos was busy during the months of May, June, and July. Barrels of flour, salted meat, water, and firewood were carried aboard the three ships and stored in the holds. Extra nails, rope, anchors, and sailcloth were stashed away as well.

A great deal of food and equipment would be needed for the one hundred twenty men scheduled to sail on the three ships. Ninety were common sailors. Several were deck officers. A surgeon, a physician, a representative of the crown, several personal servants, and a troop of soldiers completed the group.

By early August, all was ready. The men began carrying their possessions onto the ships. Ordinary seamen brought all their worldly goods in sacks. Officers brought sea trunks containing charts, navigational instruments, and armor.

One important task remained. The voyage must be dedicated to God and put under his protection.

Very early in the morning of August 3, all the crew members took Communion. Most thought it would be their last Communion ever. Then a procession of priests and altar boys wove their way through the narrow streets from the church to the waterfront.

At the rear was the bishop, who prayed, "In the name of the Holy Trinity, I place the *Niña,* the *Pinta,* and the *Santa María* into the hands of God Almighty."

At dawn the three ships set sail. A shout rose from the

Living quarters

Late in the thirteenth century, the introduction of a castle or superstructure on the aft or rear deck provided living quarters for the captain and important passengers. Later a smaller, covered area called the forecastle or fo'c'sle was provided in the ship's bow for ordinary seamen.

crowd who had gathered to see the mad admiral leave. As the three caravels began moving slowly away, the cheers turned to wailing. The women of Palos were weeping for their husbands, their sons, their brothers. They thought they would never see them again.

But the Admiral of the Ocean Seas stood proudly on deck, peering westward. There he would find the promised islands. There he would achieve his dream.

Sir John de Mandeville

When Sir John de Mandeville, an English knight, accidently killed a man, he vowed to walk around two-thirds of the earth in repentance for his sin. For thirty-five years he traveled across Europe to Jerusalem, across the Himalayas to India, eventually reaching China. When he at last returned, old and tired, he wrote his famous book, *The Travels,* published in 1357. By Columbus's time the book had been published in many languages and had become one of the most popular books of the century. Unfortunately, each time the book was translated, the stories grew more horrifying. There were stories of magnetic rocks that drew ships to their doom, tales about places in India or China whose inhabitants were cannibals, one-eyed, one-legged, or headless. There were Amazons, dragons, unicorns, gold-digging ants, and even a hand that emerged from the tomb of St. Thomas to give pilgrims Communion! Artists heightened the thrills with grotesque illustrations. Anticipating such terrors, it is no wonder that few sailors cared to venture into the unknown.

CHAPTER FIVE

Christopher Columbus Discovers a New World

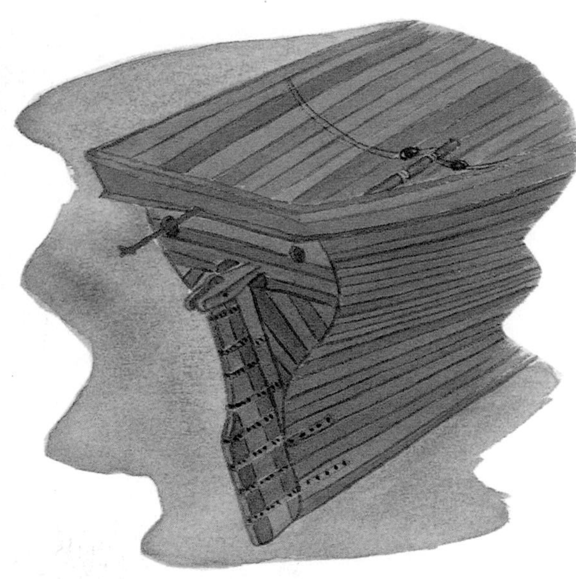

The ship's rudder
From earliest times, ships were steered by a sweep or long oar set on one or both sides of the craft. The invention of the stern rudder was a major advance in marine design. First employed in the thirteenth century, it hung from a post at the ship's stern and could be handled by a single pilot. The rudder provided greater mobility for the ship.

From the first hour at sea, Columbus recorded each event in his journal. He would first head south by southwest toward the Canary Islands, he wrote, where he would take on fresh water and other necessities. Then he would turn west and sail toward Japan.

The tiny fleet had been at sea only three days when the *Pinta* sprang a leak, and her rudder came loose. Could some frightened sailor have tampered with the ship on purpose, hoping to halt the voyage?

After waiting nearly ten years, Columbus was in no mood to turn back. "Send a man over the stern," he ordered, "and let him secure the rudder with leather thongs."

This accomplished, the three ships continued south along the African coast. After two weeks they arrived at Gomera, one of the Canary Islands. There they repaired the rudder, replaced some of the sails, and took fresh provisions aboard.

Before daybreak on September 6, 1492, thirty-four days after leaving Spain, the three ships slipped out of Gomera's harbor and headed west toward the unknown horizon. Sailors began to weep and groan as the islands' volcanic peaks disappeared from sight. What horrible fate might await them? Would they fall over the edge of

BUSCH

The captain's log

Reckonings or computations by the ship's officers were written on a slate. At the end of every four-hour watch, the information was transferred to a logbook, which was made of sheepskin. Then the slate was wiped clean.

Calming the sea

During the first voyage, the waves became tremendous such as had never been seen before. When Columbus prayed, they subsided. The sailors were amazed. Columbus said, "That high sea was very necessary for me, because such a thing had not been seen since the Red Sea drowned the Egyptians as they pursued Moses, who was leading the Israelites out of captivity."

the earth? Would a sea monster swallow their ships?

It would be another thirty-six days before they found out.

Terrified Sailors

Columbus was not frightened. He had waited his whole life for this moment. He tried to reassure his trembling crew.

"Do not be afraid," he told them. "We are safe in God's hands!" When these words had no effect, he added, "Remember, you will be rich. Think of the treasure you can bring home to your wives and children." But the sailors found sea monsters easier to imagine than gold and pearls.

To reduce their fears, Columbus decided to keep the distance they sailed a secret. He kept two separate logs. In one he recorded the actual distance covered each day. This he locked in his sea chest. The other log, open for all to see, recorded a smaller number of miles traveled.

Soon the sailors had a new reason to be afraid. The *Santa María*'s compass began to act strangely. Rather than pointing north, it was off half a degree each day. As the variation increased, the sailors began to whisper among themselves, "Is this the work of Satan?"

The admiral explained what was happening. "There are actually two norths," he said, "a magnetic north and the true north. This is not magic, but a natural law."

After many days at sea, the ships encountered a lake of seaweed stretching as far as the eye could see. Again the sailors were filled with terror. Columbus explained, "This is the Sargasso Sea, and the seaweed is only a few inches deep. We are in no danger, thanks be to God."

One night a shower of meteors shot through the sky, and the crew panicked. Once again Columbus calmed their fears, saying, "This is a common sight in southern waters. It will not harm us."

Throw the Admiral Overboard

After several weeks of strong easterly winds, the three ships arrived in tropical waters. The ocean was smooth as glass. The sailors could see the sandy bottom, coral growths, and colorful fish. The wind died down and the ships' sails flapped aimlessly.

The bell rang out for twilight prayers. The sailors assembled on deck, removed their knit caps, and bowed their heads. Above the lapping of waves on the wooden hulls, their deep voices rose in a hymn. Then all but the watchmen and the helmsmen retired to the sleeping quarters.

But that night, no one slept. Mutiny was in the air. A sailor with a patch over his eye growled, "We haven't seen land for weeks. This voyage is doomed. Let's throw the admiral overboard and head home."

"How?" asked an older man. "This wind blows only one way." The sailors looked at each other in despair. They had no idea how to steer against the wind. They had no hope of ever going home again.

Columbus learned what was troubling them. "At different latitudes," he explained, "the wind blows in different directions. If we head north to the thirty-eighth parallel, the west wind will take us home."

His explanation calmed the fears of some. But others continued to grumble and utter threats against the admiral.

An Important Decision

On October 4, a flock of migrating birds flew over the *Santa María*. Columbus knew this was a sign that land was near. He announced, "Queen Isabella has offered a purse of ten thousand maravedís to the first man to sight land. Keep a sharp lookout, for I am certain we shall reach the Indies at any moment."

But in his heart, he was concerned. According to his secret log, they had already sailed more than two thou-

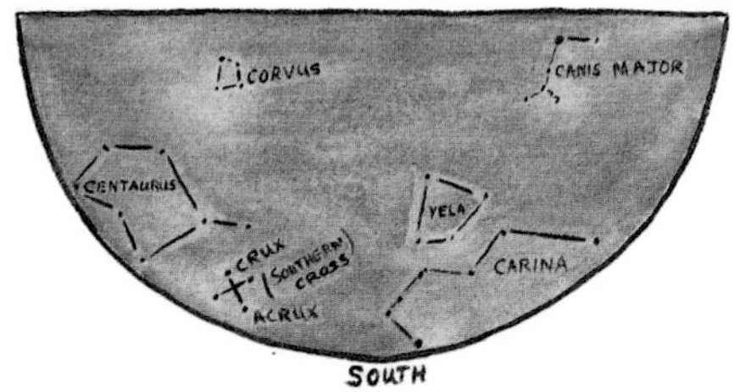

The Southern Cross

The North Star is not visible below the equator. Mariners in the southern hemisphere sight on the Southern Cross, a group of four stars, to locate their position. The Southern Cross lies over the south pole.

Cooking at sea

Each of Columbus's ships carried a firebox on deck for cooking. Each noon, the sailors burned firewood in this sand-filled metal box and used it to prepare hot meals. Cured meats and vegetables were cooked in a stewpot. Bread could be baked in the firebox, too. Live animals were carried on board to provide occasional fresh meat and eggs. The firebox never was used during rough weather for fear of setting the wooden ship on fire. Then the crew ate hardtack, or dry biscuits.

A warm reception
When they first saw Columbus's ships, the San Salvador natives thought the sails were wings. They believed the ships were great birds from heaven, and they thought the sailors were gods. At each island, the natives would run to the shore and shout, "Come and see the men from heaven!"

The first discovery
Most historians agree that San Salvador, whose name means "Holy Savior," was the first island Columbus discovered. The native name for this island was *Guanahani.*

sand miles without reaching land. What was wrong?

The admiral retired to his cabin to pray.

Four days later, on October 8, Columbus signaled for the officers of the three ships to assemble. The Pinzóns rowed to the *Santa María* and joined Columbus at his chart table.

The four men pored over their maps. They made computations, considering the winds, tides, and distance covered. The Pinzóns recommended, "Let us sail two hundred leagues farther. If we find no land, we will turn back rather than suffer a mutiny or loss of all hands."

Reluctantly, Columbus agreed.

On October 9, one of the Pinzón brothers saw land birds flying southwest. He recommended that the ships change their course to follow the birds. Columbus agreed and gave the order.

Land Ahead!

Two nights later, on October 11, Columbus saw a flickering light through the velvet darkness. Afraid his imagination was playing tricks on him, he summoned the pilot. "Can you see anything over there?" he asked.

The pilot hesitated, then whispered in amazement, "Sir, it looks like a moving fire." But as suddenly as it had appeared, the light was gone. Fearing to disappoint his disgruntled men, Columbus decided to say nothing until morning.

But at 2:00 A.M., a cannon boom broke the night's stillness. This was the signal if land was sighted. Columbus shouted, "All hands on deck! Drop the sails and lay to." The three ships rocked gently in place until daylight.

On Friday morning, October 12, as dawn lit the sky, Columbus made out the form of an island six miles away. He could see its glistening white beaches bordered with dense forests. The three ships moved toward it.

Suddenly naked men with painted bodies raced to the water's edge and waved at the ships. *Could this be Japan?*

Columbus wondered. *Why is it populated by savages? Where are the golden temples and great palaces?*

He ordered his men to launch the longboats. Then, dressed in his finest velvet cloak, the Admiral of the Ocean Seas stood tall and proud in the bow of the longboat and raised high the flag of Castile and Leon.

Stepping onto the beach, Columbus fell to his knees and kissed the ground. His entire company did the same. Everyone was grateful to God that their perilous journey was over. Everyone was thankful to be alive.

San Salvador

Rising, Columbus drew his sword and took possession of the land in the names of King Ferdinand and Queen Isabella of Spain. He called the island *San Salvador,* in honor of the holy Savior who had brought them safely to the new land.

The Spaniards were fascinated by the natives, with their straight black hair and reddish skin. Supposing he had landed on some remote island of the Indies, Columbus called them Indians. In his journal he wrote, "I believe they could easily be made Christians. I will bring some of them to the king and queen so they can learn our language and be baptized."

The sailors were now ashamed of their plots against Columbus. They fell down on their knees before him, kissing his hands and asking forgiveness. The admiral forgave them readily, but he required each of them to take an oath of obedience. As governor of this new land, he did not want to risk mutiny again.

In his report to Ferdinand and Isabella, Columbus wrote, "It is the Almighty God who gives to all who walk in his way victory over things apparently impossible."

The victory was Spain's, but it was also Christopher Columbus's. Through his unflinching faith in God and confidence in his own calculations, he had made a great discovery.

Columbus meets the natives

This is how Columbus described the first natives he saw on San Salvador: The natives were naked, beardless, with straight black hair which was coarse and falling to their shoulders. Their faces and bodles were painted red, black, and white, giving them a wild appearance. Their complexion was tawny or copper. They were well proportioned, of moderate height. The men who came to greet him were around thirty years old with high, broad foreheads and fine eyes. They were gentle and friendly and had no iron tools.

Religious services on board

Columbus held three private religious services each day on his ship. At these services, he prayed and read from the Bible. The services were held at seven o'clock in the morning, two or three o'clock in the afternoon, and dusk. In addition, the entire crew sang vespers on deck.

Looking for Gold

The first day on San Salvador, Columbus noticed that the natives wore small pieces of gold in their ears and noses. Could this have something to do with the golden streets and palaces he had read about in Marco Polo's book? Using gestures, he asked them where the gold came from.

The chief pointed southward. He added that fierce warriors lived there, and that their king lived in a golden palace.

At last, thought Columbus, *I am on the track of the Great Khan. China cannot be far away.* He ordered his men back to the ships. "I want to see where this gold comes from," he said. "With the Lord's help, I cannot fail to find it."

The ships sailed past the many small islands in the Bahama chain. Then they came to a much larger island, which we now call Cuba. It was as big as England and Ireland together, and it had high mountains.

After finding a safe harbor, Columbus sent his captains into the interior. They returned with a glowing report. "We saw yams under cultivation, beautiful singing birds, pink flamingos, and many kinds of delicious fruits we had never tasted before."

This was not what the admiral was waiting to hear. Where was China? Where were the islands of Japan with their gold-roofed pagodas?

No Gold in Sight

An old native told one of Columbus's officers that there was gold deep in the island's interior. Columbus sent two men and a native guide to find it. "When you meet the Great Khan," he told them, "tell him we come in peace, bearing greetings from the king and queen of Spain."

The envoys discovered a village inhabited by over a thousand people. Their chief welcomed and fed them. The Spaniards were amazed to see natives rolling up leaves, lighting them with a firebrand, puffing on them,

Animal life
Rats, pigs, cows, horses, dogs, and cats were not native to the islands of the West Indies. The only existing wildlife were rabbits, iguanas, birds, and fish. Researchers know when Europeans visited an area because of the presence of animal bones previously unknown to the region.

Food
For food the native Americans cultivated the yucca root, maize (corn), and potatoes. They also hunted coneys, iguanas, and various birds; and they fished. In addition, they enjoyed fruits planted in groves and grapes growing wild everywhere.

and blowing smoke from their mouths and noses. But there was no sign of gold.

When the men returned with no gold, Columbus was very disappointed. All the natives could tell him was that the gold was farther south. He decided it was time to set sail.

Far in the distance loomed an island topped by a range of mountains. Columbus headed toward it. There, on the island he would name Hispaniola after his adopted country, he would find gold. He would also lose his flagship.

Columbus had already lost the *Pinta*. Martín Alonso Pinzón, its captain, had disappeared November 24, taking his ship and some crew members with him. Columbus was hurt and angry, but he was too busy with other things to chase them.

Farewell, *Santa María*

Now it was Christmas Eve. The two remaining ships were on the way to Hispaniola. Columbus had been awake for twenty-four hours, directing the ships past dangerous rocks and shoals. He called to his captain, "Tomorrow I plan a hard day exploring this island. I place you in charge for now so I can retire to my quarters and rest."

But the captain wanted to celebrate the holiday with his mates. The night was calm, and he asked the inexperienced cabin boy to steer the ship.

Suddenly the admiral was thrown violently out of bed. The *Santa María* had run aground and was lodged on the coral reef encircling the island!

Columbus ordered the longboat lowered and a rope attached to the ship's bow. Men in the boat would try to pull the ship free. "Row, row harder, men!" he shouted. "We've got to free our ship!"

But no matter how hard the men pulled on the oars, the *Santa María* would not budge. The wind rose. Heavy surf broke hard against the ship, pushing it even more

Native gods
The natives of Hispaniola believed in one Great Spirit born of a woman. They also had many small stone or wooden gods called *Zemes*. The Zemes, crafted to look hideous and frightening, were kept in huts for protection. People constantly asked them for their help.

Horses
Many Native Americans feared horses. They thought they were ferocious beasts who would devour their enemies. Some thought the horse and rider were one creature, and they drew pictures that resembled Greek centaurs (half man and half horse). Columbus was not afraid of the natives in the interior of Hispaniola: on his second voyage, he brought horses along with him.

Canoe paddles
Caribbean natives used canoe paddles that resembled the large wooden paddles used by bakers to remove bread from a hot oven. Some of these paddles have been discovered preserved in bogs. Similar paddles are still used in the Bahamas today.

Hanging skulls
The Spanish explorers thought the American natives were cannibals because they strung human heads and limbs from the rafters of their huts. But these were actually remains of deceased family members. Keeping a part of the body nearby was the natives' way of honoring a loved one.

firmly onto the rocks. Finally her beams split open, and the proud ship turned on her side.

As Christmas dawned, it was obvious that the ship was a complete loss. The sad admiral ordered his men to remove everything of value. Natives came in their canoes to help. Everyone worked together, and the wet and damaged materials piled up all over the beach.

What should they do next? Columbus and his captains saw that there was plenty of good wood in the *Santa María*'s hull. They decided to build a fort. Sailors pried the boards loose and floated them to the beach.

In a few days, they had completed a good-sized fort with a moat and towers. They named the place La Navidad, "The Nativity," because they had arrived there on Christmas Day.

Gold at Last!

It was now January 4, time to return to Spain. Columbus chose thirty-nine men to remain at La Navidad and guard the fort. The rest of the two crews would have to crowd aboard the small *Niña.*

Harsh winter winds churned up the ocean, and the little caravel had to wait several days. One day a sailor spotted familiar sails in the distance. "Look!" he shouted. "There's the *Pinta!*"

The runaway ship pulled alongside the *Niña,* and Pinzón came aboard. The treacherous captain was full of excuses. The winds were contrary, he said. He was forced into the open sea.

In truth, he had been searching for treasure. Unlike Columbus, he had found large quantities of gold. He kept half for himself, and he divided the rest among his crew, all friends or relatives.

But at least the *Pinta* was back, and Columbus now had two ships for the return journey. He sent men ashore to cut firewood and fetch water. While they were filling the casks, they finally found what they were looking for.

Gold glistened on the sandy river bottom! Gold stuck

to their hands and feet! Gold clung to the sides of the water barrels!

Columbus was jubilant.

Time to Leave

At last the winds were favorable, and Columbus set sail. At first the two ships cruised along the Hispaniola coast. When they came to a large bay, they dropped anchor and the men went ashore for water.

Suddenly they were attacked by a fierce band of Carib Indians! The natives shot at the Spaniards with bone-tipped arrows and struck them with war clubs.

Up to now, Columbus's men had met only peaceful natives. They were shocked at this hostile reception. And they were equally surprised the next day when the Carib chief came to Columbus, smiling and bringing presents.

The admiral was pleased, and he invited the chief on board the *Niña*. There he gave him some trinkets from Spain. Delighted, the chief told him, "There is another island, richer in gold and pearls. It lies that way." He pointed east, toward Puerto Rico.

Always ready for one more try, Columbus ordered the anchors raised. But he had sailed only a few miles when the wind changed. He told the captain, "This wind is from the south. It is what we need to return to Spain. I think it's time to stop exploring. We must head home while the weather is in our favor."

The captain agreed. The crew began to shout, "Home! Head home!" Slowly the two ships turned and began the long voyage back to Spain. It was January 16, 1493.

Weapons
The native Americans used bows and arrows with great skill, both for hunting and for war. When Carib men left their villages to fight elsewhere, the women took up bows and arrows to protect themselves and their families. Even the most skillful American archer, however, was no match for European guns.

Gunpowder
Gunpowder was first used in European weapons in the fourteenth century. Spanish guns and cannons could easily overpower primitive spears and bows and arrows. Now a handful of Spaniards could subdue entire tribes in the New World.

CHAPTER SIX

Christopher Columbus Returns in Triumph

Columbus's coat of arms
Every nobleman in Columbus's time had a crest, or coat of arms, that represented important events in his family's history. Columbus was not born a nobleman, but he appreciated being honored. King Ferdinand granted his request for a title and gave him a coat of arms. His crest contained the royal arms of Castile and León—the castle and the lion. It showed the islands he discovered surrounded by water. The motto read, "To Castile and León, Columbus gave a new world."

The voyage back to Spain was easy right up to the last week. The ships set a northeasterly course to the thirty-eighth parallel. Then they turned east and let the strong westerly winds blow them toward Europe.

The admiral had kept a careful record of winds and currents so he could retrace his route. He knew how to use the best charts and instruments of his day. And his sense of direction was so good that his crew thought it was supernatural.

By February 12 his pilots estimated that the two ships were only a few hundred miles west of Spain. Actually they were headed for the Azores, islands about nine hundred miles west of Portugal.

Disaster Strikes

Suddenly they were struck by a violent winter storm. The caravels were tossed about like corks on the mountainous waves. Blinded by sheets of rain, the pilots lost sight of each other. For the second time, the *Pinta* disappeared.

The storm lasted for many terrible days and nights. Columbus feared his little ship was doomed. The devout admiral retired to his cabin to pray. His crew vowed that if they were spared, they would make a pilgrimage, walking barefoot, to the first church they saw.

Certain that the *Niña* would sink, Columbus wrote a letter describing his discoveries. He put it in a barrel and tossed it overboard, hoping someone would find it and break the news of his wonderful discovery. But that would not be necessary.

After several days of battling howling winds and lashing waves, the pilot shouted, "Land ahead!" He had sighted Santa María, the southernmost island of the Azores.

On February 18 the ship reached land. Most of the crew immediately disembarked and looked for a church so they could fulfill their vow. But the Portuguese townspeople were afraid of these strange Spaniards. They surrounded the exhausted sailors and took them prisoner.

Learning of this new disaster, Columbus raised anchor and put out to sea with a skeleton crew, leaving the would-be pilgrims on shore. Three days later he returned to the island. Anchoring offshore, he was pleased when the longboat appeared with his missing crew. The Portuguese, finding them harmless, had set them free.

On February 24, Columbus and all his men set sail once more.

.S.
.S. A .S.
X M Y
Xpo FERENS

Columbus's unique signature
Columbus believed he was elected by God to discover the New World. He thought he had been set apart from all mankind. He therefore invented a signature unlike any other. *XRO* is Greek for "Christ"; *ferens* is Latin for "bearer." The letters just above his name stand for "Jesus, Mary, Joseph." The next line up may be for "save my soul," and the top *S* may be for "Savior."

Spain at Last

The *Niña* scudded before the wind as more storms tossed her about, ripping her remaining sails to shreds. On March 4, the admiral found himself at the mouth of the Tagus River, near Lisbon, Portugal.

The news of the admiral's successful voyage spread quickly. People came out to the *Niña* in boats, shouting up their praises to the discoverer and hoping for a glimpse of the Indians that had come back with him.

Columbus stayed in Portugal just long enough to call on King John II, who had laughed at his plans many years before. He did not want to miss this chance to tell the king about the New World and show him the strange inhabitants, animals, and plants he had brought back with him.

Then the *Niña* set sail for Palos, Spain, the crew's home port. To Columbus's surprise, so did the *Pinta*. It had survived the storm after all, but Captain Pinzón was terminally ill from the stresses of the voyage. He died within the week.

The residents of Palos went wild with joy at seeing their relatives alive. While they celebrated, the Admiral of the Ocean Seas was making plans to go to Barcelona, where Ferdinand and Isabella were holding court. It was time to report on his voyage. He was eager to show the six Indians, the exotic plants and fruits, the gaily feathered parrots, and the prancing monkeys.

Columbus had written the king and queen from Lisbon, and they were awaiting his appearance with great expectancy. When he arrived at the port of Barcelona, he received a tumultuous welcome.

New World flora and fauna
Wherever Columbus went in the Americas, he collected specimens of plants, animals, seeds, and fruits to take back to Spain and show the king and queen.

A Hero's Welcome

Quickly news of Columbus's voyage reached every town and hamlet in Spain. As the admiral rode a white stallion through Barcelona, crowds thronged to see him. Bells pealed and people gathered to see the spectacle. Nobody wanted to miss the red men with painted faces!

Everywhere Columbus was greeted with pomp due a lord. He was followed by a large retinue of nobles, knights, and clergy. They had forgotten their former disbelief and mockery. Now they applauded Spain's greatest hero.

A platform was erected outside the cathedral in Barcelona's main square. Ferdinand and Isabella were seated on their thrones under a golden canopy emblazoned with their initials and coats of arms. There Ferdinand expressed to Columbus the gratitude and praise of the entire nation.

Columbus stood tall and proud. He had suffered many insults from kings, priests, and scholars, but now they respected him. He approached the throne and prepared to bow before the royal pair. But Ferdinand raised him

Natives with tails
When Columbus returned from his first voyage, he wrote in his report to the Spanish monarchs that some natives were alleged to have tails. In 1564 French artist Jacques Le Moyne showed the likely reason for these reports. He painted Timucuan Indians in festival dance costumes decorated with foxes' tails.

Thanks be to God!
Columbus recorded that, on his second voyage, he celebrated each discovery by singing two hymns: *Te Deum,* or "We Praise Thee, O God," and *Salve Regina,* or "Hail, Holy Queen."

Conquest or conversion?
Columbus wrote to the governor of an island: "I charge you above all to observe the greatest justice and discretion in regard to the Indians, protecting them from all wrong and insult, keeping in mind their majesties were more desirous of the conversion of the natives than of any riches to be derived from them." Margarite totally disregarded these instructions. Natives were burned alive. They had both hands cut off, were hung with their feet almost touching the ground, were starved and beaten and worked to death.

up. "Sit beside us," he said to the pleased admiral. Then the king gave Columbus a coat of arms, making him a nobleman.

Remembering his vow, Columbus told Ferdinand and Isabella that he would use a portion of his wealth from the New World to free the Holy Sepulcher in Jerusalem. He promised to furnish an army of fifty thousand soldiers and four thousand horses to fight against its Muslim captors.

Later the grand cardinal of Spain honored Columbus with a banquet. At the banquet, a jealous Spanish courtier challenged the foreign-born admiral. "If you had not found those islands," he said, "any Spanish captain might have made the discovery."

Columbus did not reply directly. Instead he said, "I invite anyone here to stand this egg on end."

All the banquet guests tried to do so without success. Finally Columbus struck the egg on the table, flattening one end, so that it stood without falling over. "I also showed the way to the New World," he said. "Nothing is easier than to follow."

The Second Voyage

The Spanish monarchs were eager to learn more about the places Columbus had discovered. They decided to send him back to make further discoveries, to convert the natives, and to find more gold.

The queen especially wanted to convert the natives to the Christian faith. She sent twelve priests, and she gave articles of worship from her chapel to be used in the New World. Before leaving Barcelona, the natives Columbus had brought back were baptized in the great cathedral.

No time was lost in preparing a great fleet for the second voyage.

Columbus assembled seventeen ships from every port in Spain. An immense store of muskets and longbows was available for the expedition, since they were no longer needed to use against the defeated Moors.

With no one left to fight, restless knights and adventurers by the thousands begged to join the expedition. Many offered to pay their own way. In the end, fifteen hundred men were chosen for Columbus's second voyage.

As the huge fleet set sail from Cádiz on September 25, 1493, Columbus, now forty-two, stood on the deck of his flagship gazing toward the west. He had enjoyed the praise and thanks he had received from adoring Spaniards. But even more, he looked forward to returning to the beautiful islands he had discovered.

Columbus in Chains

It would be nice if Columbus's story could end right here. The explorer was happy. Spain was exuberant. And a vast new world was opening up. But, sadly, not everyone shared Columbus's high ideals.

Many greedy people went with him on his second voyage. They were not interested in seeing beautiful lands, proving scientific theories, or making the natives Christian. Instead they hoped to gain gold, land, and slaves.

They set the natives to work in fields and mines far from their villages, without adequate food or shelter. Thousands died, and the natives stopped trusting European explorers.

The second voyage was a big disappointment to most of those who hoped to get rich, and when Columbus made his third voyage, in 1498, few men offered to go with him. He filled his six ships with criminals. Fights broke out wherever the explorers went.

In addition, Columbus tried to convert the natives through force rather than love. Five shiploads of natives were taken to Spain, supposedly so they could be instructed in the Christian faith. When they arrived, they were sold as slaves.

Columbus appointed governors in the cities he founded, and some of these men were cruel. If the na-

Pineapple

It was during Columbus's second voyage that he and his men tasted pineapple for the first time.

The tragedy of Fort La Navidad

On his second voyage, Columbus anchored off La Navidad, where he had established a fort and left soldiers in charge. He fired two cannons to alert the people of his arrival. No reply came. On landing, he discovered soldiers' corpses tied to stakes in the form of a cross. The fort lay in ruins, burned and sacked, with broken chests and ragged remnants of European clothing strewn about. Several shallow graves contained the remains of more soldiers. Suspecting the local tribes were responsible, Columbus went to their village. But it, too, had been sacked. Eventually he found the chief in another place. He had been wounded, and he claimed the destruction was the result of a Carib attack.

Line of demarcation
Pope Alexander VI wanted to avoid conflict between Spain and Portugal while the New World was being explored. In 1493, he defined a line stretching from pole to pole 370 leagues west of the Cape Verde Islands. All territory discovered east of this line would belong to Portugal, and all lands west would belong to Spain. When Europeans agreed to this line of demarcation in 1494, no one even considered that the lands rightfully belonged to the natives, not to the explorers.

tives rebelled against these heavy-handed leaders, they were massacred.

Back in Spain, Columbus had enemies who were jealous of the honors he had received. They hoped to cause his downfall. They eagerly gathered up any complaints coming from the New World and reported them to the king.

As the king's representative in the New World, Columbus was held personally responsible for anything that went wrong: uprisings of the Spanish criminals who accompanied him, torture and massacre of Indians, even insufficient quantities of gold. Everything was Columbus's fault.

Disgrace and Sorrow

Ferdinand was already disgruntled. His new territories had rapidly become a financial burden. They were not providing the boundless wealth he had hoped for. He ordered Columbus's arrest and imprisonment.

It was a bad time for Columbus. Almost blind, he was racked with fevers and suffered painful gout. Still, he was chained and led to the very ship he had so recently commanded.

During the long voyage home, the great discoverer was harassed by the rough sailors, who enjoyed seeing him humiliated. Back in Spain, he was charged with cruelty to the Indians and oppressing settlers of the New World colony. His titles and honors were stripped from him.

Queen Isabella, however, came to his rescue. Shocked at Columbus's pitiful appearance, she ordered his chains removed. She asked to hear his side of the story. Moved to tears, she restored his titles and rank.

But Columbus never again wore the velvets and brocades of a Spanish don. Perhaps he knew in his heart that his mission as Christ-bearer to the Indians had failed. The Spanish conquerors had brought the gentle natives only suffering, slavery, and death.

From that time on, Columbus, sick at heart, wore the

Magical eclipse
One week before it happened, Columbus prophesied that the sun would be darkened on February 29, 1504. He knew that there would be an eclipse on that date. He had figured this out from astronomical tables kept on his ship. When the eclipse occurred, the natives were so terrified of Columbus's "supernatural abilities" that they obeyed his every wish thereafter.

rough brown habit of a penitent—a person who is repenting of his sins.

Honored Again

In 1502 Columbus left on his final voyage to the New World. This time his second son, Fernando, age thirteen, went with him.

He anchored at the Isthmus of Panama and explored inland, never realizing that only a few miles away was the vast Pacific Ocean and, on the other side, the Orient.

He also sailed up the Orinoco River of Venezuela, not suspecting it was on a new continent. Columbus thought it was an extension of Asia.

King Ferdinand took no notice of Columbus's further discoveries. He even refused to receive the admiral at court.

Two years after returning from his fourth voyage, on May 20, 1506, Columbus died in Valladolid, Spain. His last words were those of the Savior: "Father, into thy hands I commend my spirit."

Columbus never realized he had discovered a new hemisphere and two continents. He died a broken man. But today his fame continues to grow. For Columbus stands out in history as a man of vision and courage who never gave up faith in his venture. He believed his mission was holy, and he relied on God's power to make his voyages of discovery possible.

Progress comes only when someone is willing to try what has never been done before, no matter how many people say it can't be done. Such a person was Christopher Columbus. Five hundred years after his great discovery on October 12, 1492, he will once again be honored by the entire world.

Hawk's bells

During his fourth voyage, Columbus came to an island with three peaks. He named it *Trinidad* for the Holy Trinity. The natives there wore many strings of pearls about their necks. He gave them beads, brass, and bells. They especially liked the bells, which had previously been used on the feet of trained hawks who hunted game birds.

Rest in peace

After his elaborate funeral in 1506, Columbus was buried in the Franciscan monastery in Valladolid. In 1513, his remains were transferred to Seville's Carthusian monastery. Twenty-three years after that, the remains of both Columbus and his son Diego were taken to the Santo Domingo Cathedral. After another move to Havana, Cuba, the remains were returned to Santo Domingo. In 1940 the Columbus Memorial Lighthouse was erected on a cliff overlooking the sea. This spot is believed to be his last resting place. After so many moves, however, no one is absolutely sure where he is buried.

RESOURCES

Some Other Books about Columbus and His World

Columbus, Christopher. *The Journal.* Translated by Cecil Jane. New York: Bramhall House, 1970.

Columbus, Ferdinand. *The Life of the Admiral Christopher Columbus.* Translated by Benjamin Keen. New Brunswick, N.J.: Rutgers University Press, 1959.

Foster, Genevieve. *The World of Christopher Columbus.* New York: Charles Scribner's Sons, 1963.

Irving, Washington. *The Life and Voyages of Columbus.* New York: Thomas Y. Crowell, 1828.

Koenig, Marion. *The Travels of Marco Polo.* New York: Golden Press, 1964.

Landstrom, Bjorn. *Columbus.* New York: Macmillan Publishing Co., 1966.

Las Casas, Bartolome de. *The History of the Indies.* Translated and edited by Andree M. Collard. New York: Harper and Row, 1971.

Letts, John. *Sir John Mandeville: The Man and His Book.* New London: Batchworth Press, 1949.

Marx, Robert F. *Following Columbus: The Voyage of the Niña II.* New York: World Publishing Company, 1966.

———. *The Treasure Fleets of the Spanish Main.* Cleveland, Ohio: World Publishing Company, 1968.

Morison, Samuel E. *Admiral of the Ocean Sea.* New York: Little, Brown, and Company, 1942.

Orlandi, Enzo. *The Life and Times of Columbus.* New York: Curtis Books, 1966.

Severn, Tim. *The Brendan Voyage.* New York: Avon Books, 1971.

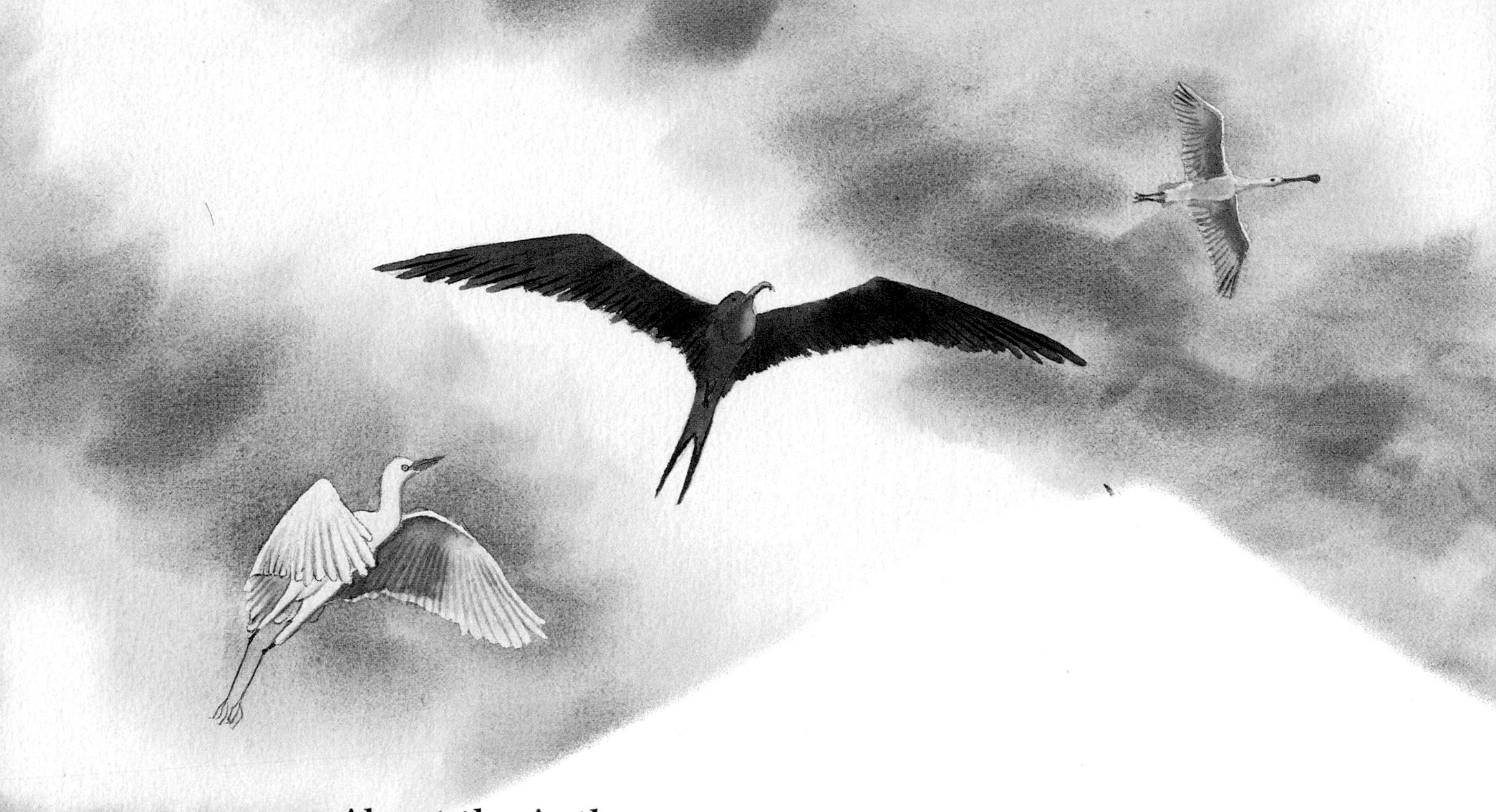

About the Author

Elaine Murray Stone, the award-winning author of eight children's books, is also an accomplished musician. She lives in Melbourne, Florida.

About the Illustrators

Pam E. Webb lives on a houseboat in the Bahamas, not far from the site of Columbus's first landing in the New World. Her original watercolors have been exhibited internationally.

Jeffrey Busch has illustrated many children's books including two recent volumes of *Classics Illustrated*. He lives in Aurora, Illinois.

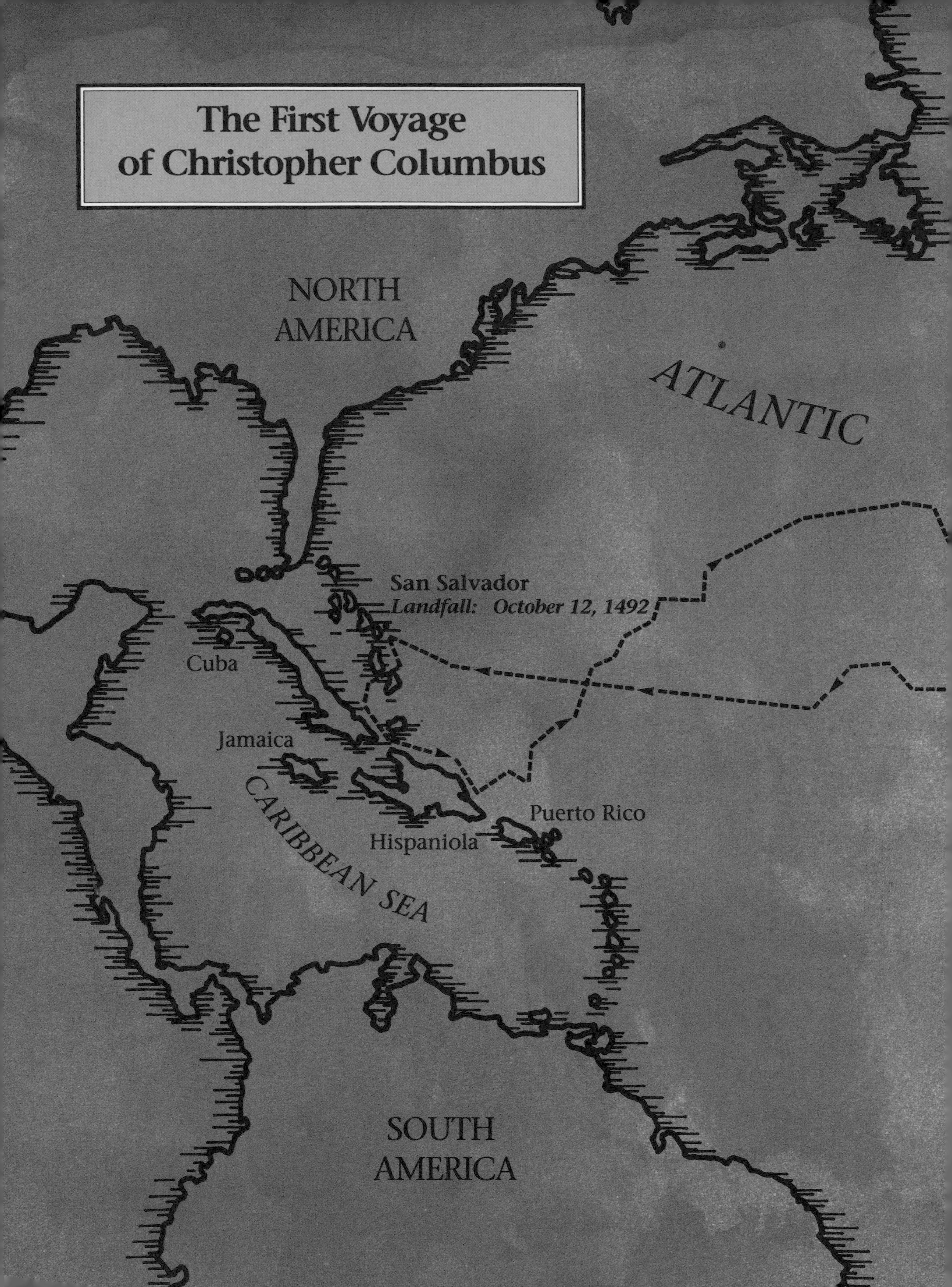
The First Voyage
of Christopher Columbus
NORTH
AMERICA
ATLANTIC
San Salvador
Landfall: October 12, 1492
Cuba
Jamaica
CARIBBEAN SEA
Hispaniola
Puerto Rico
SOUTH
AMERICA